–500–
QUESTIONS
AND
ANSWERS
ABOUT THE
BIBLE

-500-
QUESTIONS
AND
ANSWERS
ABOUT THE
BIBLE

NEIL GRANT

Derrydale Books

New York

ACKNOWLEDGEMENTS

The illustrations in this book are taken from:
The All-Colour Children's Bible, The Answer
Book of History, Children's Bible Stories from the
Old Testament (Dean), Children's Bible Stories
from the New Testament (Dean), The Hamlyn
Children's Encyclopedia, The History of the
World, The Story of Jesus, 365 Bible Stories and
Verses, The World's Greatest Wonders.

The Artists include:
John Berry, Val Biro, Bernard Brett, David
Bryant, Norma Burgin, Mike Codd, Neville Dear,
Peter Dennis, Liz and Gerry Embleton, Reg Gray,
Gwen Green, Roger Hall, Ron Hanna, Richard
Hook, Tony and Roger Hutchings, Alan Jessett,
Angus McBride, Neville Mandell, Ken Petts,
Porter, G., Sara Silcock, Chris Skilton, Gerald
Whitcomb, Michael Whittlesea.

This 1988 edition published by Derrydale Books,
distributed by Crown Publishers, Inc., 225 Park Avenue South,
New York, New York 10003.
Prepared by The Hamlyn Publishing Group Limited
Michelin House, 81 Fulham Road, London SW3 6RB

Text Copyright © The Hamlyn Publishing Group Limited 1988
Illustrations pages 138, 151, 167, 177, 180
Copyright © Neville Dear 1983, 1988
All other illustrations Copyright © The Hamlyn Publishing
Group Limited 1971, 1978, 1980, 1982, 1983, 1988

Printed and Bound in Italy

ISBN 0-517-66472-0

h g f e d c b a

CONTENTS

The
Old Testament

What is the Bible?

The word "Bible" means "the books." It is not one book but a collection of books, written over a period of about a thousand years.

The Bible contains the sacred books of the religions of Judaism and Christianity. For Jews and Christians, the Bible is not simply history, or stories telling the truth or even teaching. It is "the word of God." God has spoken and inspired many, varied human beings, and they are passing on his message as revealed to them.

The Bible is divided into two main parts, called the Old Testament and the New Testament. The Old Testament is about the relationship between God and his "chosen people," the people of ancient Israel. The New Testament, which is much shorter, contains the story of Jesus and his first disciples. The Old Testament is the Bible of Judaism. The Christian Bible contains both the Old and the New Testaments.

How did God make the world?
Genesis 1

The story of Creation in Genesis tells us how God created the world in six days. To begin with, there was nothing except endless darkness covering lifeless water. On the first day, God created light, followed by the land and sea, the sun and moon. Then he created the seasons, plants, fishes, birds and other animals. On the sixth day, God created human beings—in a form which looked like God himself.

This story is pure poetry, created thousands of years ago by a people who lived in tents among their flocks and lay at night looking up at the stars with wonder and curiosity. It is not supposed to be a scientific account of the origins of the universe.

And yet, strangely enough, the order in which things happened according to the Book of Genesis resembles quite closely that found in modern ideas about evolution.

"And God said, 'Let there be light,' and there was light."

What is the Book of Genesis about?

The Book of Genesis is a book about beginnings. The first chapter tells of God's creation of the universe, and of human beings. Genesis tells, too, how human beings became rebels and sinners, and how all of them, except for one family, were destroyed by the Great Flood.

After the Flood, another beginning was necessary. This is found in the special relationship between God and Abraham, whose descendants were the people of ancient Israel. It is this story which takes up most of the Book of Genesis.

The Book of Genesis is the beginning of the Bible, but not only because it comes first. The later books would mean nothing without the account given in Genesis of God's promises to Abraham and his descendants.

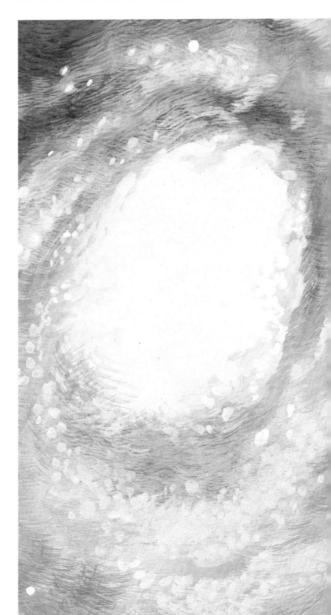

What is the Sabbath?

The story of Creation in the Book of Genesis tells us how God, when he had created heaven and earth and all living things in six days, blessed the seventh day and made it a day of rest —a holy day (or, as we say, a holiday).

"Sabbath" comes from a Hebrew word meaning "stop" or "desist." In the Jewish and, later, Christian religions, the Sabbath is "the Lord's Day." It was, and is, strictly observed by very pious people, who do not work and make no journeys except to go to worship. Jesus and his disciples got into trouble for plucking ears of wheat as they walked through a field on the Sabbath.

In Judaism, the Sabbath is Saturday. The early Christians, however, made Sunday their day of worship because the Resurrection took place on that day, the first day of the week instead of the last.

Where was the Garden of Eden? Genesis 2

The Bible tells us that when God had made human beings, he planted a garden in the land of Eden far away to the east. Later in the Book of Genesis, there is another remark about the location of Eden, when we are told that Cain went and dwelt in the land of Nod, on the east of Eden.

As this whole story is poetry rather than history, it seems foolish to wonder exactly where the Garden of Eden was, but because the writers of the Book of Genesis actually gave directions to it, though rather vague ones, it seems that they may have based their story on a real place. Great efforts have been made to discover where this place was, but without much success. However, if the writers of Genesis *were* thinking of a real place, it was probably in southern Mesopotamia, what is now Iraq (see page 19).

The fruit of the Tree of Knowledge is often pictured as an apple, although the Bible does not say that the tree was an apple tree.

What do the names Adam and Eve mean?

The name Adam, though it is also a proper name, can also mean "mankind," and it is sometimes used in that sense in the Old Testament. In Hebrew, there is also a very similar word that means "soil." (God created man, according to the Book of Genesis, out of "dust".) The name Eve means "life" or "mother of life."

What happened to Adam's rib?
Genesis 2

According to the story in Genesis, God created man first and made woman from him. He put Adam to sleep and took one of his ribs, which he built up into a woman. Afterward, God made Adam's flesh heal.

What was the Tree of Knowledge? Genesis 2

According to the account of the Garden of Eden in the Book of Genesis, God planted in the middle of the garden the Tree of Life and the Tree of Knowledge of Good and Evil. Adam and Eve were forbidden to eat the fruit of the Tree of Knowledge, but they disobeyed and thus brought about the Fall—when all humans became sinful creatures.

The story is not meant to relate something that actually happened; it is meant to teach a lesson. The lesson is that human beings, unlike all other animals, have the power of choice. Adam and Eve made the wrong choice, and suffered as a result. The writer of Genesis is saying that mankind made and goes on making the wrong choice out of pride, and so will continue suffering as a result.

What was the Serpent? Genesis 3

Eve in the Garden of Eden was tempted to eat the forbidden fruit from the Tree of Knowledge of Good and Evil by the Serpent. The Serpent, of course, is another symbol, like the Tree itself. It stands for evil desires—the kind

of temptation which we should all fight against.

We think of the creature that tempted Eve as a snake, because it is called a serpent. What the writers of Genesis were probably thinking of, however, was a mythical beast more like a dog, with a snake-like head. There are several examples of such creatures in ancient art. There was one, for instance, among the animals, real and imaginary, on the Gate of Ishtar in Babylon.

Who were the sons of Adam and Eve? Genesis 4–5

Adam and Eve had a great many children, but the two whom we know best were their first two, both sons, Cain and Abel. When they grew to be men, Abel was killed by Cain.

Why did Cain kill Abel? Genesis 4

The Bible tells us that Cain was a farmer, a crop-grower, and Abel was a shepherd. One day, they both brought presents, or sacrifices, to God. Cain brought some of the produce he had grown, and Abel brought some of his young lambs. God welcomed Abel's gift, but took no notice of Cain's.

This made Cain very angry and jealous. He lured Abel into a place in the wilds where no one could see them, and there he murdered him.

When God asked Cain where his brother was, he said he did not know, and asked the famous question, "Am I my brother's keeper?" But God cursed him and drove him away, condemning him to wander the earth as a beggar.

Cain, whose name means "smith" or "craftsman," later became a city dweller, and one of his sons, Tubal-Cain, became the first master-blacksmith.

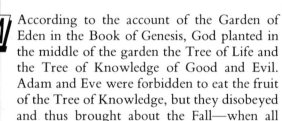

The quarrel between Cain and Abel represents the beginning of conflict and violence in human society.

What was behind the quarrel between Cain and Abel? Genesis 4

The story of Cain and Abel teaches us more about the nature of sin. Cain's jealousy of Abel led to murder, but this was a crime not only against Abel, but against God and against Cain himself. For as Cain said, everyone from then on would be against him.

The story has an historical as well as a religious meaning. Many people have wondered why God accepted Abel's present of lambs but rejected Cain's present of crops. We can assume, of course, that Cain had done something to offend God, but we are not told what this was, and it does seem that the writers of Genesis were sympathetic to Abel, rather than Cain. When we remember that they belonged to a tribe of wandering herdsmen, we can see why this was so. They identified with Abel, the shepherd, and were hostile to Cain, the farmer. Here we can see a common conflict in human history between nomadic and settled peoples. An example of such a conflict occurred in the American West in the nineteenth century when the cattle ranchers were the enemies of the homesteaders.

What was the Great Flood? Genesis 6

The story of the Deluge, or Flood, is a favorite, although in one way it is a grim one, since it tells of the destruction of most of the human race.

The descendants of Adam and Eve had increased so that thousands of people lived on earth. But since evil had come into the world, when Adam and Eve had eaten the forbidden fruit, almost all of these people were wicked, and God was sorry that he had ever created them. He decided to rid the earth of them altogether. The rain fell without pause for 40 days and 40 nights, and the water rose until it covered even the tops of the highest mountains. The only ones saved were the family of a good man, called Noah, whom God had warned in time for him to build a boat. On board the boat, according to God's instructions, were two of every kind of animal—one male and one female.

All these survived the Flood, even though the water did not begin to go down for 150 days. Then the human race and the animals began again.

The story seeks to show, in vivid picture form, that God is good and hates evil. He will punish it but will look after those that remain true to him, and forgive those who sin. It uses the common symbol of a Flood to stand for destruction, and includes many other delightful touches, such as the raven (then considered an unclean bird), the dove (considered gentle), and the rainbow (the storm is over, the sun is coming out and God smiles again).

Who built the Ark? Genesis 6

 The word *ark* comes from the Hebrew for a box or chest, and it means a kind of houseboat. It was built by Noah and his sons, Shem, Ham and Japheth who, with their wives, escaped the fate of the rest of humanity when the earth was covered with water during the Great Flood.

According to the story in Genesis, God gave very precise instructions for building the Ark. The ribs of the hull were to be made with cypress wood, and it was to have a thatched roof, a door in the side, and three decks—upper, middle and lower. God even supplied the measurements.

When was the Flood?

Stories about a great flood are found in the literature of other ancient peoples. Early civilizations were founded in river valleys, so floods were in any case quite frequent events. One account survives, engraved on a clay tablet from ancient Babylon; it is part of the Epic of Gilgamesh, going back over 4,000 years.

Many of the details in the Babylonian story are very similar to the one in the Bible. The one main difference is the presence of God, as an all-powerful but human-like being, in the Bible story. The gods (they had many of them) in the Babylonian version are pictured as a quarrelsome, fearful lot, who scramble over the sacrifices offered by Gilgamesh in thanks for deliverance like flies over a carcase.

Many scholars have tried to prove that there was indeed one great flood, which gave rise to all the different stories. However, although archeologists have found evidence of serious

floods in several places in the Middle East, these seem to have happened at different times. Although the Flood can probably be placed in southern Mesopotamia, it is impossible to give it a certain date.

 How did Noah learn that the Flood had gone down? Genesis 8

 The Ark eventually grounded on Mount Ararat (in present-day Turkey), but Noah and his family, sealed up inside, did not know if the Flood had drained away. Noah had made a trapdoor in the Ark, however, and through it he released a raven to see if the land was dry. The raven flew around above the Ark, but there was nowhere to perch. After waiting a week, Noah sent out a dove. Like the raven, the dove came back to the Ark, having found nowhere to settle. After another week, Noah sent the dove out again. This time it returned with a fresh twig from an olive tree in its beak, a hopeful sign. After another week, the dove was sent out again, and this time it flew away out of sight and did not return. Noah threw open the door and looked out. The earth was dry.

 Why did Noah's sons mock him? Genesis 9

 There is another story about Noah in the Book of Genesis. Although it comes just after the story of the Flood, it seems to be about a different man.

Noah and his family settled down again after the Flood, and his sons became the ancestors of all people on earth. Noah, says the Bible, was a farmer, and he began to plant vineyards. But he drank too much of the wine he produced and became drunk. His sons mocked him. This seems most unlike the man whom God had saved, alone among the human race, because he was such a good man.

Perhaps it shows that even a good man, when he has a completely new start, does not always remain faultless.

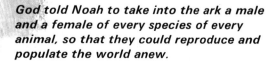

God told Noah to take into the ark a male and a female of every species of every animal, so that they could reproduce and populate the world anew.

17

Q How old was Noah?

A The Book of Genesis records that Noah was 950 years old when he died. This was not unusual for the Patriarchs who are listed in Genesis. Methuselah, who, according to Genesis, was Noah's grandfather, lived even longer, 969 years.

Of course, we are not supposed to take these immense life-spans as true. There is no reason to think that people lived any longer in ancient times than they do now. In fact, most of them died much younger. The reason for giving the ancient ancestors such long lives was probably that the writers of Genesis believed in a kind of golden age before the Flood, when everything was splendid and went on more or less for ever. (Some of the ancient Babylonian kings were said to have reigned for thousands of years. Nobody was counting the years in those days.)

Q Why was the Tower of Babel built? Genesis 11

A The story of the Tower of Babel gives one explanation for the different languages spoken by different people. Babel, the Hebrew name for Babylon, was indeed a place where many languages were spoken. Like other stories in Genesis, the story is also about the nature of sin. In this case, the sin is pride. By building a tower that would reach heaven, the builders put themselves on the same level as God. The result was, as always, disastrous for the sinners, resulting in confusion and exile.

Today, archeologists believe they have found the remains of the Tower of Babel. It was a tall ziggurat—a building like a pyramid but with stepped sides—which was associated with the worship of the Babylonian god Marduk.

Q How were bricks made?

A The book of Genesis tells us that the builders of the Tower of Babel used bricks.

The best building material in ancient times was stone, but in Mesopotamia, this was hard to come by. Therefore bricks were used instead. They were made of mud—and there was plenty of that in the area, thanks to the flooding of the rivers—bound together with chopped

straw, baked hard in the sun and held together with bitumen, or pitch, as mortar. The earliest bricks were made by hand, but later they were made in wooden molds, so that they all came out the same size and shape. Some of the earliest houses in the Middle East were made of mud bricks which, in a dry climate, will last a very long while.

Who founded Israel? Genesis 11–25

Abraham, stories about whom make up a large part of the Book of Genesis, is regarded as a founding father by no less than three religions —Judaism, Christianity and Islam. In the Bible, he is the ancestor of the people who became the Hebrews or the children of Israel.

Scholars have argued at great length about whether Abraham, or Abram as he is also called, was an historical person or not. Some believe that he was not an individual but the symbol of a tribe. He certainly appears as a very individual character in the Bible. Other scholars used to think that the stories about Abraham and his wanderings were nothing but myths. But modern archeologists are finding that the account of Abraham's movements is likely to be true.

In any case, the point of the stories about Abraham, and many of the other old stories in the Bible, is not to tell an exact history but to show God's great plan which lies behind history.

**Left, the Tower of Babel
Below, the wanderings of Abraham, from
Ur to Canaan**

Where is Mesopotamia?

The ancient land of Mesopotamia is roughly the same as modern Iraq, though in the Bible the name is given to a smaller region. Through it ran the "twin rivers"—the Tigris and the Euphrates—and the plain through which they flow was one of the earliest, probably *the* earliest, centres of civilization. In Lower Mesopotamia, the Sumerian civilization flourished, to be succeeded by Babylon, while the home of the Assyrian empire was in Upper Mesopotamia, in the north.

Mesopotamia had an enormous influence on Palestine, because from there came knowledge, inventions and ideas, over a period of many centuries, which were far in advance of neighboring regions.

Who were the Patriarchs?

A patriarch is the founding father of a long family line. In the Bible, the long lists of men born between the time of Adam and Eve and the time of Abraham are called the Patriarchs, but the important ones are Abraham and his immediate successors: his son Isaac and grandson Jacob (as well as, sometimes, the twelve sons of Jacob from whom the Twelve Tribes of Israel were descended).

Abraham, Isaac and Jacob lived during a period from about 1900 to 1600 BC, which is sometimes called the Patriarchal Age. At that time, most people, including the Patriarchs themselves, seem to have lived a partly nomadic life in a region ranging from Egypt to Mesopotamia, although there were already many settled areas in that region.

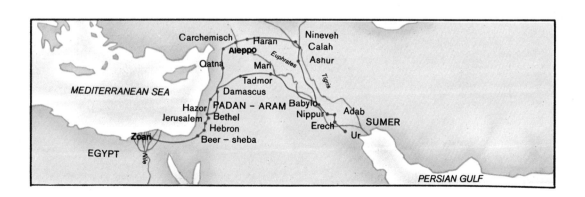

Where was Abraham born?

Genesis 11

The Bible tells us that Abraham's family came from Ur of the Chaldees, a city in southern Mesopotamia. From there they moved to Haran, in Syria, where they remained for some years before Abraham and his wife set out on their travels, which brought them eventually to the Land of Canaan (Palestine).

It is a little surprising that the founder of a nomadic, tribal people should have come from Ur, which was a city with a long history. By the time of Abraham's birth, somewhere between about 2000 and 1700 BC, the city of Ur was well over 1,000 years old. If Abraham's family were really city people, it would be unusual for one of them to take up the wandering life of a herdsman, even a rich one as Abraham became. There are no other links between Ur and the people who became the Hebrews.

What were the earliest homes of the Israelites?

Abraham, who lived before about 1700 BC, was a tent-dweller, and it was not until more than 500 years later that nearly all the Israelites settled down in permanent houses and villages.

The tents of the Israelites probably looked very like those still sometimes used by Arab herdsmen today. They were long and low, slightly higher in the middle than at the sides, and straight-sided. In Abraham's time, they were made of animal skin, but later the usual material was woven goats' hair, which is nearly waterproof and also resists heat. It does shrink when wet, but that could be an advantage because it shrinks itself tight.

Tents continued to be used long after the Israelites had become town-dwellers. People were nostalgic about the nomadic, tent-dwelling life just as we are about village or country life.

The Apostle Paul was a maker of tent cloth by trade.

Where was the Land of Canaan?

Abraham and his people settled in the Land of Canaan on God's instructions. Later, after his descendants had wandered far away, Canaan became the Promised Land to which they would one day return: "the land flowing with milk and honey."

In the Old Testament, the name Canaan was given to a district covering most of the land between the River Jordan and the Mediterranean Sea, from Syria in the north to Egypt in the south.

In the hard years of wandering, the Israelites looked forward to a life of plenty in the Promised Land.

What are nomads?

People are called nomads when they have no fixed home, and live by wandering with their flocks of animals from place to place, searching for grazing and water. In Abraham's time, the people who became the Israelites were nomads, living in tents which could be easily packed up when it was time to move on.

There are several different kinds of nomads, and it seems that, even in Abraham's day, the Hebrews were making some moves toward a more settled life. The Bible tells us of shrines—permanent buildings—being built and wells being owned (you cannot very well "own" a well unless you live near it). We hear, too, of conflicts with settled people over grazing rights and water supplies. In the hot, dry summers, when grass and water were scarce, such clashes were bound to happen since the nomads were forced to live along the edges of settled land, moving from one watering place to another.

Were the ancient Hebrews Bedouin?

When we think of Middle Eastern nomads today, we think of Bedouin, a name which means "man of the desert." There are still a few Bedouin left in Arabia, moving from one oasis

Camels were not used by nomads until much later than the time of Abraham.

to another with their camels.

"Camels" is the important word here. Bedouin are camel-breeders; the camel is the centre of their life and work. But at the time of the Biblical Patriarchs, camels were still entirely wild animals. They were not domesticated until about 1200 BC. Abraham's people were therefore not Bedouin.

What was the wilderness?

There are many references in the Old and New Testaments to "the wilderness." Sometimes the word "desert" is used instead, and we often think of it as a bare, lifeless expanse of sand.

But that is not quite what the Hebrew word that we translate as "desert" or "wilderness" means. A closer translation would be "deserted land," the land where no one lives. It meant an area which, for one reason or another (but mainly lack of rainfall), was no good for farming and not even fertile enough for nomadic herdsmen, except for a short spell in the wetter part of the year. No trees grew in the wilderness, and in that respect it was very different from what the colonists called "the wilderness" in North America, meaning regions of thick forest.

What was God's name?

In the Old Testament, several words are used to describe God, such as "the Almighty" or "the Lord," but strangely enough, we do not know for certain the name of the God of the ancient Hebrews. It was considered disrespectful to say or write God's name, and instead the Hebrew writers put only four consonants—**J** (or **Y**), **H**, **V** (or **W**), **H**. When the Bible was first translated into English in the Middle Ages, the vowels **E**, **O** and **A** were put in, giving the name Jehovah. We now know this was a mistake. The name should be Yahweh, pronounced *Yar-way*.

According to the Book of Exodus, the name Yahweh dates from the time of Moses. It is said to mean, "I am that I am," or "God is one who exists and can never cease to exist."

What is the meaning of the Covenant?

After the Flood, God made a covenant with Noah, in which he promised never again to destroy all living creatures with a flood. Later, God made a covenant with Abraham in which he gave the Land of Canaan to his descendants.

A covenant is an agreement, a contract, between two people or, in this case, between God and his people. It is a kind of blending together of the wishes of the two parties involved, an agreement on a common course of action. It involves commitments on both sides.

The idea of the Covenant is very important in the Old Testament; in fact, it can be said to be the underlying theme of the main story, which is the relationship between God and his chosen people. In the time of Moses, God made a covenant with Israel—that is, with all of the people—which became the basis of Hebrew law.

Who was Ishmael? Genesis 16

For a long time, Abraham and his wife Sarah had no children, so Abraham took as a second wife a young woman called Hagar, who was Sarah's maidservant. Hagar became pregnant, but not long afterwards Sarah did too. There was jealousy between the two mothers-to-be, and Hagar ran away into the desert, though an angel persuaded her to return. She then gave birth to a son who was called Ishmael.

The Bible does not tell us much about Ishmael as a person. However, he was the supposed ancestor of the Ishmaelites, a semi-nomadic people who were relatives of the Israelites but often at odds with them and regarded by them as an inferior people. Ishmael is therefore not a very great figure in the Jewish tradition, but in Islam he is more highly regarded. He is said to be an ancestor of Muhammad, and he and Hagar are said to be buried in the most sacred Muslim shrine, the Kaaba in Mecca.

What is a sacrifice?

The original meaning of the word "sacrifice" was "to make something sacred" or "holy." Gifts were offered to a god, and as a possession of the god they became holy. In the earliest times, sacrifices were supposed to provide God (or the gods) with food, though later they became symbolic, like the communion in the Christian Church. In the original form, a sacrifice was a holy meal eaten either by the gods or by the gods and the worshippers. A

common kind of sacrifice was the "peace offering," in which the blood of the sacrificed animal was poured on the ground, the fatty parts were burned on the altar, and the meat eaten by the worshippers. Only certain animals could be sacrificed. Lambs were probably the most common.

Q **Is the Bible a history book?**

A Unlike most religious books, the Bible is not just a collection of religious teachings; it is also the story of the people of Israel. The Old Testament covers a period of roughly 1,000 years, while the New Testament, whose purpose is different, adds about another fifty years.

Some of the events and persons in the Old Testament are mentioned in what survives of other ancient literature. Some can be linked with the discoveries of modern archeology.

However, it is impossible to make a satisfactory "time chart" of the Old Testament, or of the life of Jesus as narrated in the New Testament. The reason is that, although the Bible contains much history, it is not a history book. The Bible is not intended to be a record of events: it is a witness, or a testimony, of faith in God and the way that faith changed people and events.

The idea of offering sacrifice was a common one in early religions.

23

How did God test Abraham?
Genesis 22

In God's covenant with Abraham, the promise was made that Abraham's descendants should flourish and live in the Land of Canaan. In return, God expected total obedience from Abraham, and it was to test that obedience that he put him to the test.

Whatever was sacrificed to God had to be the best, but this time God demanded more than the finest lamb. He told Abraham that he must sacrifice his son and heir, Isaac. Although human sacrifices were not usually performed by the Israelites, they were common among certain other peoples.

Abraham was so obedient to God that he would have carried out his command. But as he raised the knife to strike his beloved son, God stopped him. He had passed the test. Instead, a ram caught by its horns in a bush, and not Isaac, became the sacrifice.

What language was the Bible written in? When was it written?

The words of the Bible—especially those of the Authorized Version, or King James Bible—are so well known that it is easy to forget that the Bible was not written in English! But, of course, the Old Testament was written in Hebrew, which was (and still is) the language of the people of Israel. The New Testament, however, was written in Greek, which, 1,900 years ago, was the language of educated people everywhere in the Mediterranean area. Some parts, however, may have first been written in Aramaic, which was the common local language in Palestine in Jesus's time.

The New Testament was written in the same century as Jesus lived—though some years after him. The Old Testament, which describes things that happened between about 1900 BC and 500 BC, was mostly written some time after the events described took place. For instance, the story of Abraham and Isaac must have happened about 1,000 years before it was written down.

Who was turned into a pillar of salt? Genesis 19

Abraham's nephew, whose name was Lot, appears quite often in the stories about Abraham in Genesis. He was clearly a much less noble character than his uncle, although he was a man of honor.

Lot eventually settled in the city of Sodom, which was near the south of the Dead Sea.

Formations like this, made almost entirely of salt, can be seen south of the Dead Sea today.

Sodom and the neighboring city of Gomorrah had a very evil reputation, and God sent two angels to destroy Sodom. However, Lot, who had taken the angels in to lodge with him, was warned by them. He and his family were told that they should flee at once and should not stop to look back. Lot's wife disobeyed; she did look back and was immediately turned into a pillar of salt—one of the strange formations which can be seen around the Dead Sea (still known today, in Arabic, as the "Sea of Lot").

Archeologists have discovered evidence of a great earthquake about the 19th century BC, which might have been responsible for the destruction of the "evil" cities of Sodom and Gomorrah.

How did Isaac gain a wife?
Genesis 24

God had promised Abraham that his descendants would become a great nation. Yet Abraham had only one heir, Isaac, who, even though he was middle-aged, had still not found a wife. It was essential that he get married,

ful girl called Rebekah, and she gave him the right answer. It turned out that she was a distant cousin of Isaac, which was ideal, and after arrangements had been made with her family, she returned to Canaan with the steward and married Abraham's son.

How long did people live in Old Testament times?

The Book of Genesis lists the Patriarchs who, it says, lived for several centuries. Of course, this is not to be taken as plain fact. There is no reason to think that people have ever lived longer than they do now.

It is often said that, in former times, before the development of modern medicine, hygiene and so on, people did not live as long as they do now. This is true of the *average* life-span, which among the ancient Hebrews was probably below 40, about half what it is now. However, a healthy person, who was lucky enough not to catch any disease or to have any accident, would have lived just as long as a healthy person today. The Bible says a human life-span is "three score years and ten," which is 70. The life expectancy of a man in Europe or North America today is just about that. (Women live rather longer).

otherwise Abraham's line would die out. Of course, there were plenty of unmarried girls to be found in Canaan, but Abraham wanted his son to marry one of his own people, someone who worshiped the true God. So Abraham called his steward, his most trusted servant, and sent him to the district of Haran, where Abraham's people had settled after they left Ur and before he had set out on his travels.

The steward did not know how to go about selecting a wife for his master's son, but he prayed to God to give him a sign. He would go to the well and ask any suitable girl if she would give him a drink. If she gave a certain answer, the steward would know she was the one God had chosen. He asked the question of a beauti-

Archeologists are all the time increasing our knowledge of the Biblical past.

How did Jacob cheat his brother?
Genesis 27

 Isaac had two sons. Although they were twins, Esau was the older, and therefore he was his father's heir. But the younger son, Jacob, was the smartest. One day, when Esau was very hungry, Jacob managed to cheat him out of his right of inheritance in return for a bowl of soup. Later, aided by his mother, Rebekah, whose favorite son he was, Jacob cheated Esau out of his father's blessing. This blessing was much more than a symbolic act: something of Isaac's soul went into Jacob when he blessed him, and that was why, once the blessing had been given, it could not be given again to Esau, to whom, as the first-born son, it was due.

There are several things in the story of Esau and Jacob which seem rather strange, but this is another case where we are being told some history, with nations disguised as individuals. Esau was the ancestor of the people of Edom, the nation closest to Israel, who spoke the same language. Israel—or, in this story, Jacob—despised the Edomites but also feared them.

 Who was the ancestor of the Twelve Tribes of Israel?

 When Jacob was on his way to Haran, in search of a wife from Abraham's stock (like his father before him), he stopped for the night at a place he afterward named Bethel. While he slept, he had a dream. He saw in his dream a ladder, its feet on earth, rising up into heaven. Angels were going up and down it, busy on God's errands. God stood beside Jacob in his dream. He promised to give the land on which he lay to Jacob and his descendants, who would be as numerous as the grains of dust.

According to tradition, Jacob was the ancestor of the Twelve Tribes of Israel, which were descended from his twelve sons.

 Why did Jacob marry two sisters? Genesis 29

 In Haran, Jacob went to work for his uncle (Rebekah's brother), Laban. He fell in love with Laban's daughter Rachel. He was not able to marry her for seven years, owing to some local custom, but as the Bible very beautifully says, the seven years seemed like just a few days

Above, When Jacob reached Haran he met Rachel, his cousin, at the well, where she was watering her flocks, and fell in love with her.

because he loved her so much. During that time, he worked for Laban.

When the wedding at last became possible, Laban tricked Jacob into marrying not Rachel but her sister, Leah, because she was the elder daughter and it was the custom for the elder daughter to marry first.

However, it was not unusual for a man to have more than one wife in those times, and Jacob later married Rachel. Although Jacob loved Rachel, it was Leah who was the mother of six of his twelve sons.

Left, Jacob deceives his blind father and thus receives the blessing intended for his older brother, Esau.

How did Jacob marry the wrong girl?

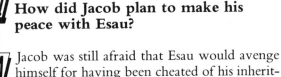

Jacob wrestles with the angel.

Several other civilizations, besides that of ancient Israel, have stories about men who marry the wrong women. Sometimes it is the result of too much celebration before the wedding—the bridegroom is so drunk, he cannot see whom he is marrying. The Bible suggests that Jacob did not realize he had been given Leah instead of Rachel because it was dark. There was, however, another reason: until the day after the wedding ceremony, the bride would have worn a thick veil, and it would have been impossible to see her face. It may still seem rather unlikely that a man could marry the wrong woman by mistake, but it was not impossible.

Jacob but Israel. Jacob then continued on his journey, and he was limping because of his dislocated hip.

This is a strange story in some ways. It is like a common folktale about a traveler who outwrestles a demon, but it is more than that. It probably results from two or three stories being put together at different times. It signifies Jacob's change of character: he had previously been a rather crafty and untrustworthy fellow, but afterward he became a noble Patriarch. However, the precise meaning of "Israel" is not known. It probably means "May God rule," not "He who struggles with God," as the story seems to suggest.

Who wrestled with Jacob? Genesis 32

After some time, Jacob argued with his uncle Laban and set off to return to the Land of Canaan, where his father Isaac was still living. One night, after Jacob had decided to stay in a quiet place to be by himself, a strange man appeared and challenged him to wrestle. They wrestled all through the night, and when the man found he could not overcome Jacob, he struck him so hard on the thigh that Jacob's hip was dislocated. Even then, Jacob would not let the man go until he gave him his blessing.

The stranger, who is assumed to be a messenger of God, or an angel, asked Jacob his name, and then told him it would no longer be

How did Jacob plan to make his peace with Esau?

Jacob was still afraid that Esau would avenge himself for having been cheated of his inheritance and his father's blessing. So on his way back to the Land of Canaan, Jacob decided to bring a present for his brother and chose 220 goats, 220 sheep, 30 camels, 40 cows, 10 bulls, and 30 asses from his own herds to give to Esau. This inventory may seem a bit doubtful—Jacob, who must have lived about 1700 BC, would probably not have had either camels or cattle—but it does show that Jacob was a rich man.

In those days, when there was no proper

money, a man's wealth was his herds. The more animals he had, the wealthier he was, and the wealthier he was, the more power and influence he had among his people. The herds would have been mostly sheep and goats, with donkeys for carrying the tents and baggage. The importance of sheep and goats in the lives of the Israelites can easily be guessed by the number of times they are mentioned in the Bible. Even after the Israelites had settled down in towns and villages, the herds were important to them.

What were the Twelve Tribes?

The twelve sons of Jacob became the founders of the Twelve Tribes of Israel, whose territories are shown in the map, as far as we know them.

Although the twelve sons all had the same father, they had different mothers. Only the last two, Joseph and Benjamin, were the sons of Rachel. The first ten are generally known as the Leah tribes, but Leah was the mother of only six of them: Reuben, Simeon, Levi,

The territories of the Twelve Tribes, who were descendants of Jacob's twelve sons.

Judah, Issachar and Zebulun. Dan and Naphtali were the sons of a maid of Rachel's; Gad and Asher were sons of a maid of Leah's.

God promised to give all the tribes land—except the Levites, who had a special job as assistant priests—in what came to be known as the "Promised Land" in the time of Moses.

What are angels?

We usually think of angels as heavenly creatures, human-like but not really male or female, with a pair of golden wings sprouting from their backs and a halo over their heads. That is how most artists have portrayed them. However, "Angel" means "messenger," and an angel in the Old Testament is merely a messenger of God, who may be quite an ordinary-looking person. (If the angels Jacob saw in his dream had had wings, they would not have neeeded a ladder to go between heaven and earth, and it is hard to imagine wrestling with a man with wings!) But angels are not ordinary messengers. They have a special authority—they speak with the voice of God. In fact, they sometimes almost seem to be God himself.

Why was Egypt so attractive to the Israelites?

Although the Israelites were, in the end, desperate to get out of Egypt and back to the land which, they believed, had been promised to them, they went to Egypt in the first place of their own free will. We know, too, that Abraham, in his day, had spent some time in Egypt.

The delta and valley of the Nile in Egypt was very fertile territory. When there was famine in Canaan, there was probably plenty of food in Egypt, and semi-nomadic people, in times of drought and hardship, naturally looked toward the green fields of the Nile region. We know that some time about 1700 BC Egypt was invaded by hungry nomads from the east, and this may be the historical fact behind the story of how Jacob and his tribe came to settle in Egypt.

31

Why did Joseph's brothers hate him?

 Although he was the youngest but one of Jacob's sons, Joseph, the first child of Rachel, was his father's favorite. The long-sleeved robe that Jacob gave Joseph—called the "coat of many colors" in the Authorized Version of the Bible—was a sign of his privileged position. The wearer of such a coat would not have to work hard in the fields, as Joseph's brothers did. It is not surprising that Joseph's brothers hated him.

Joseph made things worse by telling them of his dreams. He dreamed of sheaves of wheat, and his sheaf stood upright in the field while the sheaves of his brothers bowed low before it. In another dream, he told his brothers, the sun and moon and stars bowed to him. Even Jacob, the fond father, thought this was too much, and reprimanded Joseph. It was obvious that the sun and moon were meant as Joseph's father and mother, and the stars, his brothers.

Below, Joseph's brothers threw him into a pit, "and the pit was empty; there was no water in it."

Opposite, Pharaoh invested Joseph with symbols of his office.

Who was Potiphar? Genesis 37–40

 Joseph's brothers imprisoned Joseph in an underground water tank after Reuben, the eldest, had persuaded them not to kill him. When some merchants passed by, they decided to sell their brother as a slave. They stained his coat with blood and showed it to Jacob, who assumed his favorite son had been killed by wild animals.

The merchants who bought Joseph traveled to Egypt, and there they sold him again. He was bought by Potiphar, an important officer, who is described as Pharaoh's captain of the guard.

Potiphar's wife took a liking to Joseph, but he refused to have anything to do with her. In a jealous rage, she accused him of making advances to her, and he was thrown into prison.

What was Pharaoh's dream?
Genesis 40–41

While he was in prison in Egypt, Joseph interpreted the dreams of two of Pharaoh's servants. One of them was Pharaoh's butler, who was restored to his position three days

later. When Pharaoh was troubled by a strange dream which no one could interpret, the butler remembered Joseph and told his master about him. Pharaoh sent for Joseph and asked if he could interpret dreams, to which he replied that God showed him what the dream meant.

Pharaoh had dreamed of seven thin cows which ate up seven fat cows but grew no fatter themselves. He had another dream in which seven fat ears of corn were eaten up by seven shriveled ears.

Both dreams, Joseph explained, meant the same thing. Egypt would have seven years of good harvests, followed by seven years of bad harvests. He advised Pharaoh to appoint an official to take charge of storing up enough produce in the seven good years to see the country through the seven bad years that would follow. Pharaoh was so impressed with Joseph that he gave this job to him.

Q When did the Israelites settle in Egypt?

A The story in Genesis tells us how Jacob and his sons came to live in Egypt when Joseph became Pharaoh's right-hand man. We know that the reason for this move was hunger: as had often happened before, the semi-nomadic peoples of the east made for fertile Egypt when times were bad. There is no record of their arrival in Egypt, but that is not very surprising. They were probably not a very large group and offered no threat to Pharaoh and his people.

The Bible says that the Israelites remained in Egypt for 430 years. Archeological research has shown that this is probably quite accurate, and we can therefore calculate that Jacob and the tribes arrived in Egypt in the 17th century BC. At the time, Egypt was ruled by the Hyksos pharaohs, who were foreigners themselves and sympathetic to the Israelites, to whom they may even have been distantly related.

What is the difference between Israelites, Hebrews and Jews?

The history of the people we know as the Jews really begins with Abraham. However, we cannot properly talk about the "Israelites" until after the time of Jacob, who was renamed Israel and was father of the twelve founders of the Twelve Tribes. The name Hebrew dates from a slightly later time. It was, at first, a rather rude name given to them by the Egyptians.

Although Israelite and Hebrew usually mean the same thing, in fact the Hebrews were a much wider group, including related nations such as the Moabites and the Edomites (descendants of Esau). Hebrew is also the name of their language.

The name "Israel" can be especially confusing too, because it can be a man (Jacob), a people or the name of a Hebrew kingdom after the country had been divided in two (the other was Judah).

The name "Jew" comes from Judah, and is a later name than either Israelite or Hebrew. In New Testament times, it was often applied to those who were especially strict in religious observance, like the Pharisees.

Why were the Israelites unhappy in Egypt?

At first the Israelites did very well in Egypt. Their numbers increased enormously and they became a powerful group within the Egyptian kingdom. Many years after Joseph's death, when he had been forgotten, a new pharaoh came to the throne who was suspicious of the Israelites, afraid they might assist Egypt's enemies if the kingdom were attacked. His first plan to reduce the threat of the Israelites was to make them work very hard as slave labor on construction sites. They *were* treated very harshly, but the worse they were treated, the more their numbers increased, or so it seemed.

Something had to be done, so Pharaoh then gave the incredible orders that all boy babies born to the Israelites were to be killed at birth. (Girl babies, when they grew up, would be forced to marry Egyptian men, so they were not considered a threat.)

Who was the baby in the bulrushes? Exodus. 2

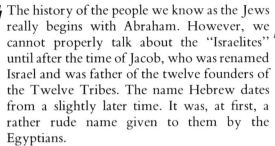

Pharaoh's order that all boy babies among the Israelites should be killed was widely disobeyed. One woman succeeded in hiding her baby for three months, and she then thought of a clever scheme to make sure he was brought up safely. She hid him in a reed cradle which she floated in the river, near the spot where Pharaoh's daughter bathed. She told her own daughter to keep watch.

When Pharaoh's daughter came down to bathe, she noticed the floating cradle and sent her slave girls to fetch it. She was surprised and delighted when she saw the baby boy inside. She knew that he must be a Hebrew child, but she decided to keep him. She called him Moses because it meant "to draw out," and she had drawn him out of the water.

There are, of course, many stories in the folklore of other peoples about babies abandoned in the wild and brought up by someone else.

Who was paid for looking after her own baby?

When Pharaoh's daughter found the baby Moses in the bulrushes, she decided to keep him. Moses's sister, a grown girl, was still watching, as her mother had told her, and she could see Pharaoh's daughter admiring the baby. So she went up to her and asked if she should find a Hebrew woman who would look after the baby. Pharaoh's daughter agreed and, naturally, the girl went to fetch Moses's mother. Pharaoh's daughter told her that she would pay her wages if she looked after the baby until he was old enough to be taken into her own household. This is what happened, and Moses became like Pharaoh's daughter's own son.

Why did Moses fly from Pharaoh's court? Exodus 2

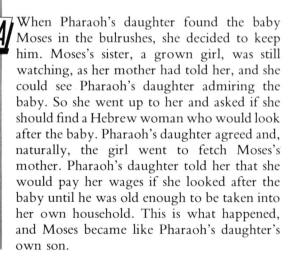

Moses lived as an Egyptian prince but he never forgot that he was a Hebrew. He saw how badly the Egyptians treated them. One day

The baby Moses is discovered.

when he saw an Egyptian beating a Hebrew particularly fiercely, he grew angry and killed the Egyptian and hid his body.

But Moses soon realized that people knew what he had done, and when Pharaoh found out too, Moses knew he must fly from the kingdom. He went to the land of Midian where in time he married and became a shepherd.

How did God summon Moses?
Exodus 3

When Moses was living in Midian, looking after his father-in-law's flocks, he came to a place called Horeb, a holy place in the wilderness. There, the Bible says, he saw a burning bush which, though apparently in flames, was not being burned away. Moses was bewildered, and he went to look closer. Then the voice of God called to him.

God told Moses that he had seen the misery of his people in Egypt, and that he would bring them into the land of Canaan, as he had promised. Moses was the chosen leader.

Many clever explanations of the burning bush have been put forward, but whatever actually happened—an effect of the sunset, a dream—is not important. What is important was God's call to Moses to lead his people out of slavery, which marks the beginning of the career of the greatest human figure in the Old Testament. He is also thought by some to be the author of the first five books of the Bible.

What gods did the Egyptians worship?

The biggest and the most vital difference between the religion of the Israelites and the religions of nearly every other early society was that the Israelites worshiped only one God, the all-powerful Yahweh, (see page 22).

The Egyptians, who in almost every other way were the most advanced people in the world, worshiped a large number of gods, many of which were half-human, half-animal. There were at least 800 of them, although most of them were not very significant. One that was extremely important was Ra, the god of the sun, who "died" every night and was "born again" every morning.

How did Moses turn the water red? Exodus 7

After God had identified himself to Moses and commanded him to lead the Israelites out of Egypt, Moses and Aaron confronted the Egyptian king. As Moses had been brought up in the household of Pharaoh's daughter, it was probably not difficult for him to get an audience with the ruler, but it did no good. Pharaoh refused to let the Israelites go, and he even told his men to treat them more harshly. He was not impressed by Moses's talk of the Israelites' God, and suggested that Moses and Aaron perform some miracle. Moses turned his staff into a

Moses lifted his rod, "and smote the waters that were in the river, and all the waters were turned to blood."

serpent, but as the Egyptian priests could also do this trick, Pharaoh was still unimpressed.

The next morning, Moses confronted Pharaoh on the banks of the river. Since he refused to let the Israelites go, Moses said, he would stretch out his staff over the water, whereupon it would be turned into blood.

He did so, the water turned red, the fish died, and no one could drink from the river.

Who was Aaron?

Aaron was Moses's brother and his assistant in the campaign to force Pharaoh to let the Israelites leave Egypt. He was the better speaker, and Pharaoh regarded him as co-leader with Moses. Later Aaron came to be regarded as the founder of the Hebrew priesthood. Although his name is often mentioned in the Old Testament, he is always overshadowed by Moses. The one time that he did take a more active role was in the story of the Golden Calf, but he did not come out of that story very well.

What were the plagues of Egypt?

When Pharaoh refused to let the Israelites leave Egypt so that they could worship God under Moses's leadership, Moses warned him that God would bring plagues upon his country. There were ten altogether: first was the turning of the River Nile's water to blood, continuing with a plague of frogs and ending with the deaths of the Egyptians' firstborn children and firstborn animals.

All these plagues can be understood by considering conditions in Egypt over 3,000 years ago. It is not necessary to think they were magic. Some of the plagues are clearly connected, but Moses, who knew the Egyptians well, was skillful at playing on their superstitions. For example, the disease that killed off the Egyptian cattle was probably caused by the large numbers of dead frogs lying around after the plague of frogs.

In Old Testament times, all disasters of this kind were believed to result from the action of the gods. Some people still believe this.

Why did the Egyptians fear darkness? Exodus 10

The ninth of the ten plagues of Egypt was the plague of darkness. At God's command, Moses stretched out his hand toward the sky and it became pitch dark throughout Egypt for three days. Today we think the cause of this was a dust storm.

To us, this does not seem nearly as dreadful as many of the other plagues, but to a people who worshiped the sun, it was as terrible as anything they could imagine.

What do the Jews remember at Passover?

Before the last of the plagues of Egypt, God issued instructions to the Israelites through Moses. For seven days they were to eat unleavened bread—that is, bread that contains no yeast—and on the seventh day there was to be a feast in honor of God. On that day, each man had to take an animal from his flocks and slaughter it. Some of the blood had to be put on the doorposts of the houses where the meat was to be eaten. No one was to leave the house till morning, for during the night, God's destroying angel would pass through the countryside and the firstborn in every family would die. But the angel would note the houses where blood had been smeared on the doorposts and would *pass over* them.

Everything happened as Moses predicted, and this event, the Passover, has been remembered as an important Jewish festival ever since.

It is not difficult to see that two different stories have been combined here. The unleavened bread and the slaughter of an animal are ancient harvest customs, going back far into prehistoric times. The story of the tenth plague, which resulted in the Israelites finally escaping from Egypt, has become connected with the older customs of the harvest.

The Hebrew name for the festival of Passover is Pesach, which means "to pass by," or "to spare." It is celebrated for eight days in the spring.

When did the Hebrews become a nation?

The Hebrews looked back to Abraham as the founder of their nation, but it is not until the Exodus—when they left Egypt—that we can really talk about a single nation. No one knows exactly who the ancestors of the Hebrews were, but they were certainly a mixture of a great many people. Among other early peoples, their blood certainly contained that of the Akkadians, Amorites and Hurrians, and there were also connections with various Canaanite peoples. At the time of the Exodus, there was also, naturally, a strong Egyptian element: two of the most important tribes were named after Ephraim and Manasseh, the Egyptian sons of Joseph. Moses himself was married to a Midianite woman.

 ## How did the Israelites escape Pharaoh's army? Exodus 13

The last plague of Egypt, which struck down the eldest child in every family, finally broke Pharaoh's resistance. He sent for Moses and Aaron in the night and told them to take their people out of the country as quickly as possible.

The whole nation set out: men, women and children plus servants, animals and anything that could be carried. They were not used to living rough. Although their life in Egypt had been hard, it had been settled; they had not lived as wandering herdsmen since the time of Jacob. They were guided on their way by a pillar of cloud during the day and a pillar of fire at night, but God did not guide them by the shortest route because that would bring them up against the Philistines, who might frighten them into going back to Egypt.

Once the Israelites had gone, Pharaoh changed his mind and set out after them with a force of specially chosen charioteers. He caught up with them by the Red Sea. Moses stretched out his arm and the sea was divided in two. The Israelites crossed on dry land. When Pharaoh's chariots tried to follow, the sea closed over them and drowned them.

"And Moses stretched out his hand over the sea: and the Lord caused the sea to go back by a strong east wind all that night."

 ## What was the Sea of Reeds?

Bible experts have given a number of explanations for the parting of the Red Sea, which allowed the Israelites to escape from Pharaoh's forces. Some say that the Hebrew name ought to be translated, not as the "Red Sea," but as the "Sea of Reeds." No reeds grow in the Red Sea, but there are plenty in the swampy area farther north, in the Nile delta. It may be that this swampy area was larger then, and this was where the Israelites crossed. They were likely to know the swamps better than the Egyptian soldiers because their homes were in Goshen, on the edge of the swampy region.

The story of the Exodus is more poetry than history. It shows God's great plan working, but not the details of historical events. We cannot say what caused the division of the Red Sea, nor explain the pillar of cloud and pillar of fire. We do know that, at the time of the Exodus (about 1290 BC), the Philistines had not yet arrived in Palestine.

What was manna?

When Moses and Aaron were leading the Israelites through the Sinai desert after the Exodus from Egypt, they ran out of food, which caused bitter complaints. Many said they should have stayed in Egypt: at least they would not have starved to death.

The next morning, when the dew had gone, a fine white powdery layer was left on the ground. The Israelites asked, "What is that?"—a phrase that in Hebrew sounds like the word "manna."

Moses explained that it was bread (i.e. food) sent by God for them to eat.

So what was it? It may have been some edible desert fungus, or it may have been the sugary substance made by a type of plant louse living in tamarisk trees, which grow in that desert. This sweet-tasting stuff is still gathered by people of the region.

Where is Mount Sinai?

According to the Book of Exodus, the Israelites had been traveling for three months when they came to Mount Sinai, by which time they had become a closely knit community. The mountain, it is said, was sacred, although it may only have become so as a result of what happened to Moses and the Israelites there.

Strangely enough, we cannot be certain exactly where Mount Sinai was, because we do not know which route the Israelites took when crossing the Sinai peninsula. One possibility is Jebel Helal, about 62 miles (100 km) southwest of Gaza. Although not a very high mountain—it only reaches about 1,920 feet (600 m)—it rises sharply from the plain and looks very impressive. However, there are several other mountain peaks which may have been the Mount Sinai of the Old Testament.

What is the Law of Moses?

Every society must have laws, and the origin of the Jewish Law was an important event in the development of the nation. The Ten Commandments given by God to Moses on Mount Sinai remained the center of the elaborate Jewish legal systems which developed later. They were first told to Moses, and later engraved on two stone tablets, which were kept in the Ark of the Covenant. The Ten Commandments are, in a sense, the text of the Covenant between God and Israel.

Of course, the Ten Commandments were not completely new. Other societies had similar laws. One Law of Moses that was very different, however, was the commandment against making images of God.

What is the Torah?

"Torah" means "law," "instruction," or "will of God." It is the name given to the first five books of the Jewish Bible (the Christian Old Testament). These books are Genesis, Exodus, Leviticus, Numbers and Deuteronomy. They are also known as the Pentateuch (from the Greek for "five books").

According to tradition, the author of these books was Moses. We do not know for certain that they were written later than Moses's time, so it seems quite possible that they were compiled under his guidance.

The Law is still read from a scroll in synagogues today.

What happened to Aaron's Rod? Numbers 17

A rod in the Old Testament is often a mark of authority. The word refers to a shepherd's rod, which was more of a long-handled club than a crook or walking stick. A shepherd, as leader of his flock, would carry one, and Moses, as leader of his people, also carried a rod, which is mentioned in connection with the plagues of Egypt. It was probably used because certain Egyptian priests carried magic wands.

Aaron's rod had a similar use. In addition, when it was left in the Tabernacle, it produced buds, flowers, and ripe almonds. This was taken to be a sign that God approved the choice of Aaron as the chief priest.

How did the Israelites carry their baggage?

Between the time they left Egypt and when they settled in Canaan, the Israelites lived a nomadic life, having no permanent home and sleeping mainly in tents. They depended on their flocks of sheep and goats for most things —not only meat and milk but many other necessities, such as clothes, tents and blankets.

The Ark of the Covenant, preceded by men playing ram's-horn trumpets, is carried in procession.

At the time of the Exodus, camels had not yet been tamed, but asses had been domesticated for many centuries. The Egyptians were the first to keep them, and their ancestor was probably the wild ass of Nubia.

Although only about 3 feet (1 m) high, the ass could carry a large amount of baggage, or could be ridden (for example, by a woman who was expecting a baby). It could also do other work, and was even used for pulling a plow.

What was the Ark of the Covenant?

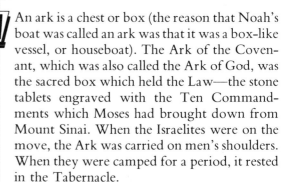

An ark is a chest or box (the reason that Noah's boat was called an ark was that it was a box-like vessel, or houseboat). The Ark of the Covenant, which was also called the Ark of God, was the sacred box which held the Law—the stone tablets engraved with the Ten Commandments which Moses had brought down from Mount Sinai. When the Israelites were on the move, the Ark was carried on men's shoulders. When they were camped for a period, it rested in the Tabernacle.

The Ark was made of gilded wood— probably acacia wood. On the gold lid, known as the mercy seat, were the gilded figures of two cherubim, or angels. It had a ring at each corner, through which rods were passed for carrying it.

What was the Tabernacle?

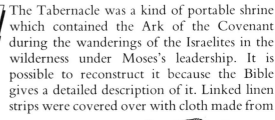

The Tabernacle was a kind of portable shrine which contained the Ark of the Covenant during the wanderings of the Israelites in the wilderness under Moses's leadership. It is possible to reconstruct it because the Bible gives a detailed description of it. Linked linen strips were covered over with cloth made from

goats' hair, which was in turn covered with skins to make it weather proof—all supported on a wooden frame. Inside it was divided into two by a veil, and the Ark was kept in the rear portion, known as the Holy of Holies. The entrance faced east, and it stood in its own enclosure, which also contained an altar for burnt offerings (animal sacrifices).

The Tabernacle

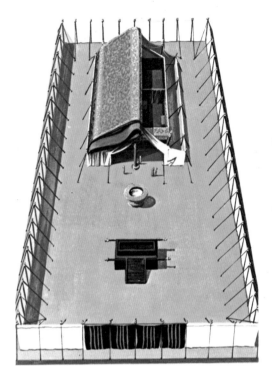

Why did the Israelites worship the Golden Calf? Exodus 32

The Bible tells us that Moses was away on Mount Sinai so long that the people lost faith in him and went to Aaron asking for a god who would lead them. Aaron melted down their gold earrings and made a golden calf which they worshiped. This was against the Second Commandment, and when Moses did return, he was so furious that he smashed not only the golden idol they had made but also the stone tablets bearing the Commandments.

The Israelites' worship of the Golden Calf shows the influence of Egypt, which they had only just left after many generations. Gold was the metal of the sun god, and animal forms played a big part in Egyptian religion. The fact that the calf was meant to represent God— Yahweh—made things worse. Hatred of idols was a powerful force in the religion of Israel: God was invisible, and it was blasphemous to try to make him visible.

Who had a talking donkey? Numbers 22

When the Israelites approached the kingdom of Moab, the king of the Moabites sent for Balaam, who was a famous seer, or oracle, living a long way off in the east. Fearing he would not be able to defeat the Israelites by force, the king wanted Balaam to put a curse on them. But Balaam at first refused to go, because God (Yahweh) had told him not to. Eventually he did go. (The story in the Bible is obviously compiled from more than one source: in verse 20 God says Balaam should go to Moab. In verse 22 God is angry when he does.)

On the way, Balaam is intercepted by an angel. He does not see the angel, but his donkey does and refuses to go on. Balaam beats it, but God causes the ass to speak, and she asks why. Finally, Balaam himself sees the angel and understands why his donkey refuses to go on.

Balaam and his ass

What is sin?

A sin is a religious crime. It is doing something against God's will, or against God's law. But it is equally possible to sin without actually *doing* anything. Sins can be committed in thought, word and deed.

All people are sinners to some extent. This is the point of the Genesis story, in which Adam and Eve, the original man and woman, committed the first sin by eating the forbidden fruit. In the Old Testament, there is also the clear idea that a whole people, or a nation, can be sinful, as the Prophets (see page 76), often told the Israelites.

The problem of sin, as the Prophets recognized, is a problem of human nature. In practice, the priests in Israel tended to regard sin merely as a matter of not obeying strictly enough the complex laws of ritual. This was merely a matter of ceremony, not morality. It was this attitude which so annoyed Jesus.

How long did the Israelites wander in the desert?

The distance from Egypt to Palestine is not very long, but for one reason or another (and partly at least because of the need to avoid battles with more powerful peoples), the Israelites took a roundabout route. According to tradition, they went way down the Sinai peninsula, through the "Wilderness of Sin." This period is mainly covered in the Bible by the Book of Numbers, which begins two years after the Exodus from Egypt and ends, 38 years later, just before the entry of the Israelites into the "Promised Land."

What kinds of animals preyed on their flocks?

In Old Testament times, there were far more wild animals than there are today, and the job of a shepherd, as protector of his flock, was more difficult and dangerous than we might suppose. Among the wild animals that could threaten the flocks of the Israelites were lions, bears, wolves, jackals and hyenas. The only weapons that the herdsmen had against mar-

auding animals were clubs or stones. Lions, however, were also a symbol of royalty and often kept in captivity.

Did the Israelites have sheepdogs?

One of the most important things in life for the people of Israel, not only when they were nomadic wanderers but also after they became settled farmers in Canaan, was their flock of sheep. The Bible is full of references to shepherds and their sheep, and Jesus often told stories about shepherds when he was trying to teach people through a parable.

One modern-day idea of a shepherd is of a man who carries a crook and works with a sheepdog, but although crooks were probably used by the Israelites, sheepdogs as we know them, were not. In those days people had different feelings about dogs. Most dogs were at least half-wild, scavengers, and perhaps carriers of disease (though that would not have been known). They were regarded as little different from jackals, not only by the Israelites but by other peoples of the region.

How did the Israelites enter the Promised Land? Joshua 3

According to the account in the Book of Joshua, the Israelites crossed the River Jordan, after the death of Moses, without even wetting their feet. The presence of the Ark had caused the river to be temporarily dammed. This meant they could attack Jericho.

Although it is not necessary to look for an historical explanation for these events (they are, in any case, rather muddled because the writer has used several different stories which do not always agree), it seems possible that the flow of the Jordan was interrupted by an earthquake, which fatally weakened the walls of Jericho at the same time. About 30 miles (48 km) above Jericho, the river runs through a narrow gorge, which has been blocked by an earthquake at least once in modern times.

The Israelites had allies among the Canaanites. Rahab was one of the most important.

Who was Rahab? Joshua 2

Rahab was a woman who lived in a house attached to the city wall of Jericho, or perhaps it was on top of the wall. When Joshua and the Israelites approached Jericho, they sent spies into the city. Rahab saved them from being captured by the authorities by hiding them on her roof. She deceived the police so the spies were able to escape out of the city again.

In return for her help, Rahab was promised that she would not be harmed when the Israelites attacked the city. However, as the city walls were destroyed, it seems that Rahab's house must have been destroyed, too, although she and her family were not. A scarlet cord was used to mark her house, we are told. But these details are not important. It is just a good story.

Rahab became something of a heroine among the Israelites. She and her family became naturalized Israelites. She is mentioned in later books of the Bible, and Matthew lists her among the ancestors of Jesus, though we cannot be certain that this is the same Rahab.

Q What is a wadi?

A A wadi is the course of a river in the desert which, however, is usually dry. It contains water only now and then, usually only after heavy rainfall, and then soon dries up again. Wadis sometimes have no obvious beginning or end. They appear in the desert, run for a certain distance, then gradually disappear again. Others begin as mountain streams, which dwindle to nothing as they run through the desert.

One example of a large wadi is the Arabah, a valley running from the Dead Sea down to one of the arms of the Red Sea, which is mentioned in the Book of Joshua and in other places. It is sometimes called the "River of the Wilderness."

Q How did Joshua conquer Jericho?

A The Israelites were already a battle-hardened people by the time Joshua led them across the River Jordan and up to the city of Jericho. However, in those times an army besieging a city had little hope of success unless they could starve the inhabitants into surrender. Jericho was very well defended by massive walls, the remains of which can still be seen today, while the Israelites had no siege weapons.

God's instructions were for the Israelite army to march around the city at regular intervals for a month. This would increase the suspense in the city. No one would know where or when the invaders would attack: no one would sleep much. On the final day, they should march round seven times, then blow a blast on the trumpets and give a great shout. This would bring down the walls—and, of course, it did. Afterward, the victorious Israelites set fire to the city.

Archeologists have found signs of earthquake and fire at Jericho. It is also possible that the walls fell down in some way closer to the method described in the Bible—as a glass can be shattered by a musical note.

The Israelites had to fight for many years before they were able to conquer Canaan, and even then they did not conquer all of it.

Q What were the trumpets of Joshua's army?

A Trumpets like those which were blown with such destructive results for the walls of Jericho, were ram's horns. They were probably the earliest musical instruments used by the Israelites, and they were sounded to give the alarm, to dismiss the soldiers and on other occasions such as, in this case, sounding the charge.

The horn, or *shophar*, was also played on certain religious occasions (as it still is).

Q Who were the Canaanites?

A The Land of Canaan, or Palestine, was larger than the modern state of Israel. It included all the land between the Mediterranean coast and the River Jordan and between Egypt and Syria, and it contained many walled cities, like Jericho. The conquest of the land by the invading Israelites took much longer than it seems to have done from the account in the Bible.

The Canaanites were, like the Israelites, a

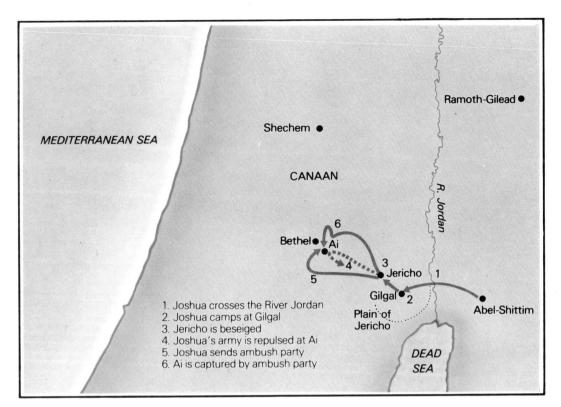

MEDITERRANEAN SEA

Ramoth-Gilead ●

Shechem ●

CANAAN

R. Jordan

6

Bethel ● Ai

3 Jericho 1

4

5

Gilgal ● 2

Plain of Jericho

Abel-Shittim

DEAD SEA

1. Joshua crosses the River Jordan
2. Joshua camps at Gilgal
3. Jericho is beseiged
4. Joshua's army is repulsed at Ai
5. Joshua sends ambush party
6. Ai is captured by ambush party

Semitic people whose ancestors probably came from Arabia.

They were only one of the groups occupying Palestine at the time of the Israelite conquest, but they were the largest and by far the most powerful. According to Biblical tradition, the Canaanites were the descendants of Ham, one of Noah's sons.

How is the history of Israel divided?

The period of over 1,000 years covered by the Old Testament can be roughly divided up into the following periods, beginning with Abraham:

* The Patriarchs (about 1900–1600 BC)
* Sojourn (settlement) in Egypt (about 1600–1280 BC)
* Exodus and Conquest (about 1280–1050 BC) including the period of the Judges (from about 1220–1050 BC)
* The Monarchy (about 1050 BC), beginning with Saul and ending with the division of the kingdom after Solomon about 922 BC.
* The Divided Kingdoms, i.e. Israel and Judah, about 930–600 BC.
* The Babylonian Exile (587–539 BC).

The map shows the probable movements of Joshua's army. The city of Ai was destroyed, but its possible ruins have been found at Et-Tell.

Why did the Israelites have to learn a new way of life in Palestine?

From the time of Abraham until the settlement in Canaan—a period of about 700 years—the normal pattern of life for the Israelites was nomadic. They moved along the edges of settled land, sometimes settling long enough to sow and reap a crop, but generally depending on their flocks for food, clothes, and shelter.

Settlement in Canaan during the Period of the Judges (about 1220–1050 BC) brought many changes. At first, people were still mainly busy with their flocks, but gradually they took over the fields and olive groves of the Canaanites, and settled in areas where there was enough rain for cultivation, though mainly in the highlands—not in the broad wheatfields of the plains which, at that time, were still held by other peoples. The Book of Judges relates the battles of the Israelites against their neighbors to take over the fertile valley regions.

Deborah inspires Barak to lead a force against Sisera.

Who were the Judges?

The Judges were the rulers of Israel between the time of Joshua and the beginning of the monarchy in the time of Samuel. They were tribal heroes and heroines, most of whom did not, in fact, "rule" a nation but led a large section of it by force of character as much as anything. Some are still famous today, including Gideon, Deborah, and Samson, though the others are less well known.

Who killed Sisera? Judges 4–5

The Israelites soon mingled with the Canaanites, but they also had to fight various peoples to make sure that their conquest of Palestine was complete. This contest went on for a long time. One of those who oppressed the Israelites was a certain king of the plains region, who had the great advantage of possessing iron chariots, as well as a fierce general called Sisera.

The leader in raising opposition to Sisera was Deborah, who is described in the Bible as both a Prophet and a Judge of Israel. She inspired a soldier called Barak to lead an Israelite force against the enemy general. Sisera was defeated, and took refuge in the tent of a woman called Jael. She, for a reason we do not know, killed him by driving a tent peg into his temple while he was asleep. An important point here, however, is that Jael acted in a particularly treacherous fashion, because she broke all the rules of hospitality by murdering someone to whom she had promised safety.

This story, incidentally, is known only from the Bible, not from archeology or other sources. There is no reason to doubt it, but we cannot tell when it happened.

What is the Song of Deborah?
Judges 5

The victory of Deborah and Barak over Sisera is celebrated in a song, or poem, which makes up Chapter 5 of the Book of Judges. It is regarded as one of the gems of ancient Hebrew literature, and is undoubtedly very old. It was probably not written by Deborah herself, but by someone who lived at the same time.

Who were the Midianites?

The Midianites were a nomadic people—in fact they can be called true Bedouin, for they seem to have been one of the first peoples to have kept camels. They appear several times in the Old Testament, sometimes on good terms with the Israelites, sometimes not. When Moses got into trouble in Egypt, he fled to the Midianites, and later married the daughter of the Midianite shepherd with whom he had taken shelter.

During the Period of the Judges, the Midianites—along with the Amalekites, another nomadic people hostile to Israel—moved into Canaan and, for a time, drove the Israelites into the hills.

The Midianites never mixed with the peoples of Palestine, as the Israelites themselves did, but kept their own individuality and their nomadic way of life.

Who defeated the Midianites?
Judges 6–8

The nomadic Midianites raided the Israelite farms and villages and drove them to seek safety in the hills. Among those they killed were the brothers of Gideon.

Gideon was a humble young member of the tribe of Manasseh, who was forced to thresh his father's grain in secret, to save it from the raiding Midianites. While he was busy at that task, an angel came to him and told him, to his surprise, that he would defeat the Midianites.

Gideon sent messengers to other tribes and raised an army of 32,000 men, but God told him that that was too many, and he reduced the force to just 300, divided into three companies.

Gideon learns of his destiny.

Their surprise night attack on the Midianite camp caused such confusion that the Midianites, thinking they were under attack by a large army, began to fight each other. The Midianites were defeated, the remnants driven off, and for the rest of Gideon's lifetime, the Israelites were no longer troubled by these enemies.

Who was Baal?

Whether there was an angel or not, it is clear that concern for his people, combined with religious feelings, drove Gideon to become one of the greatest of the Judges. The Bible's account tells us that, under God's instruction, Gideon destroyed the altar to Baal that his father had put up, and replaced it with an altar to Yahweh.

Baal, whose name simply means "lord" or "master," was the most worshiped god in Palestine when the Israelites settled there. He was chiefly a god of farming, and he was often worshiped in open fields and in high places in the hills, where offerings of crops and animals were made to him. Among the Israelites, Baal was an attractive god, and for a long time, they worshiped him as well as, or instead of, Yahweh, despite being frequently denounced by the Prophets, who strove to keep them faithful to the One God. In this struggle, the Prophets were, of course, successful in the end.

Who were the Elders?

The word "Elders" often appears in the Old Testament, and it generally means the heads of families or tribes. Such men were called "Elders" simply because they were usually men of advanced years. They were the senior members of the community, whose advice and experience were respected.

Where did the Philistines live?

The Philistines entered Palestine at about the same time as the Israelites, only from the opposite direction. They were a sea people, related to the Phoenicians (the most famous sea-going people of ancient times), and they may have come originally from south-east Europe. They were probably aiming to settle in Egypt but were driven off; instead they settled in Philistia, the coastal plain of Palestine, roughly between what is now Jaffa (then Joppa) and Gaza.

The Philistines were the Israelites' chief opponents for many years. They were very different from the Israelites in every way, with a different racial background and (of course) a different religion. They were not united as a single nation, but their city-states often acted together. Although they were the major rivals of the Israelites, the two peoples were not always at war, even if the Bible makes it seem as if they were. The Philistines were, in fact, not a real danger to the existence of Israel, and in David's time, they paid tribute to the Israelite monarchy. But they were never conquered by the Israelites.

What made the Philistines such powerful enemies?

Philistia—the coastal land occupied by the Philistines—was mostly fertile, and it was better farming country than much of the hilly regions occupied by the Israelites. It had one other great advantage: iron. At this time—the 12th century BC, when both Philistines and Israelites were establishing themselves in Palestine iron was just coming into use. The Philistines not only controlled the sources of iron,

they were also expert workers in the metal, having learned the craft from the Hittites in Asia Minor, before they settled in Palestine. Their knowledge of iron manufacture enabled the Philistines to make better weapons and tools. They were able, for instance, to put iron rims on the wheels of their chariots, and to make iron swords and spear points. That was one reason why, up to the time of David, the Philistines could challenge the Israelites, in spite of being far less numerous.

When did a donkey's jawbone come in handy? Judges 15

Samson is the last and most famous of the Judges of Israel, none of whom was a judge in our sense of the word but rather a tribal leader, and often a great warrior. Samson is the "Rambo" of the Old Testament, a figure remembered more for his brute strength than anything else, although there are other messages to be learned in the several stories of Samson in the Book of Judges.

Among the many stories of Samson's super-human strength are those of his exploits against the Philistines after he had allowed himself to be captured by them and tied up by ropes. He burst the ropes and, having no weapon, seized on the jawbone of a donkey with which he killed 1,000 men.

What was Samson's Riddle?

Besides being a man of great physical strength, Samson also had a weakness for women and—to the dismay of his family and friends—especially Philistine women.

While he was on his way to Timnath to visit the Philistine girl he wished to marry, he came upon a young lion. He killed it with his bare hands and continued on his journey. Some time later, on his way to make the girl his wife, he passed the carcase of the lion and noticed that bees had made honey in it. He took some along to his parents.

Samson could kill a lion with his bare hands.

At the wedding feast, Samson asked the young Philistine guests a riddle: Out of the eater came forth food, and out of the strong came forth sweetness. What did that mean? He promised 30 fine garments if they guessed the meaning, but they would have to give him the same if they failed.

They could not guess the answer to the riddle, but they were so anxious not to lose face that they threatened to burn the bride's house down if she did not find out its meaning for them. After some persuasion, Samson told her the answer, just as, years later, he told Delilah the secret of his strength.

What was the secret of Samson's strength?

Following the instructions delivered by an angel to his mother before his birth, Samson was brought up according to the beliefs of the Nazirites. This meant taking certain vows connected with clean living, one of which was not to cut the hair. The idea was that growing hair was the gift of God, and that it was wrong to cut it off with a man-made tool.

This was the secret of Samson's strength: he would lose it if his hair were cut. After twice fooling her with false reasons, Samson finally told this secret to the woman, Delilah, whom he loved. She told the Philistines (Delilah was probably a Philistine herself). Thus Samson fell into the Philistines' hands. He was blinded and was put to work grinding wheat in the prison at Gaza. However, when his hair grew long again, he regained his strength (it was possible to become a proper Nazirite again after breaking the vows by mistake).

Samson's final act was to pull down a house on top of an assembly of Philistine lords, killing himself at the same time. So by his own death he killed more people than he had in his whole life.

years of the settlement of the Israelites in Canaan, the Ark of the Covenant was kept there.

Bethel lay about 10 miles (16 km) north of Jerusalem, at the head of a cluster of passes through the hills of Judea. It was more exposed than Jerusalem, and was one of the first major cities to be captured by the Israelites. The story of the capture of Ai—in Joshua, Chapter 8— may apply to Bethel. Archeologists have found evidence of a city of very well-built houses destroyed by a great fire at about the time of the Israelite conquest. It suffered destruction again during the civil wars in Israel between the tribes, like the one described in Joshua (Chapter 20), when the rest of Israel made war on the Benjamites. Bethel was probably in Benjamite territory.

What tools did farmers use in Old Testament times?

The picture shows three farm tools of the kind in use before metal tools were widely made. The sickle, for severing the stalks of ripe wheat, is fitted with a cutting edge of stone. The threshing board (*top*) was a heavy, sledge-like board fitted with "studs" of stone or, later, metal, which was pulled to and fro across the wheat to separate the grain from the chaff. Grain and chaff were then flung into the air with the help of a type of rake. The breeze blew the chaff away while the heavier grain fell straight to the ground. This process, known as "winnowing," depended on a certain amount of wind to assist the process.

Why did Ruth go to Judah?

The Book of Ruth is very short and very pleasant to read, especially after all the tales of violence of the Book of Judges. It tells an attractive story of country folk, and experts regard it as a plea for racial tolerance, for the Moabites were excluded from Israel.

The Book of Ruth relates how a man of Bethlehem in Judah, with his wife Naomi and two sons, was driven by famine into the land of the Moabites, which was east of the Dead Sea. The sons married local girls, but then all three

These are some of the tools used before metal became commonly available. Their use is described in the text (right).

Where was Bethel?

Apart from Jerusalem, Bethel is mentioned in the Bible more often than any other place. The name means "House of God," and in the early

men of the family died. Ruth, one of the Moabite girls, would not leave her mother-in-law when Naomi decided to return to her own people. "Entreat me not to leave thee . . . for whither thou goest, I will go; and where thou lodgest, I will lodge: thy people shall be my people, and thy God my God."

Who was allowed to glean barley?

In the Book of Ruth we are told how Naomi and her daughter-in-law, Ruth, returned to Naomi's people in Bethlehem in Judah, arriving there at the time of the barley harvest. They had little food or money, and Ruth went out to glean the fields after the reapers, which means

for the less fortunate gleaners. In Leviticus (Chapter 19), it says "And when ye reap the harvest of your land, thou shalt not wholly reap the corners of thy field, neither shalt thou gather the gleanings of thy harvest. And thou shalt not glean thy vineyard, neither shalt thou gather every grape of the vineyard; thou shalt leave them for the poor and stranger."

How did Ruth come to marry Boaz?

It happened that the barley field where Ruth went gleaning belonged to Boaz, a cousin of her dead father-in-law. When he found out who she was, he was especially kind to her, for he admired the way she had supported Naomi

Harvesting the grain by hand was not a very efficient method. However, what was left could be "gleaned" by the poor.

she picked what was left of the crop after it had been harvested.

There would probably have been more of this than might be supposed, because it was the custom to leave a certain amount of the crop behind to be gathered by widows, orphans, and the poor. In fact, Hebrew religious law clearly stated that landowners should not harvest their complete crop but should leave some

and accompanied her back to Bethlehem in Judah although she was herself a Moabite.

It was the custom for a widow to claim protection from the nearest male relation of her dead husband and, advised by Naomi, Ruth asked for the protection of Boaz. Not only did he give this very willingly, once he had established that no one else had a better claim to protect her, he also married her. Although the Bible does not tell us, we may suspect that Boaz had loved Ruth from the time he first saw her gleaning the barley.

Ruth and Boaz had a son, Obed, who had a son, Jesse, who was the father of David.

Hannah praying at the Tabernacle in Shiloh.

 Who was Samuel's mother?
1 Samuel 1

 In the Bible, it is interesting to note how often a famous person is born to a woman who had almost given up hope of ever having a baby. Hannah, the mother of Samuel, was one such person. She went to pray at the Tabernacle in Shiloh, the religious "capital" of the Israelites in these early times, and she prayed with such enthusiasm that the High Priest, Eli, thought she was drunk and told her to go away. When she explained that she was sorrowing because she could not have a child, Eli spoke kindly to her and blessed her. Not long after, she found she was expecting a baby, and the baby turned out to be a boy whom she called Samuel, the last of the Judges and the first of the Prophets, whose name means "name of God."

 Why did Samuel go to the Tabernacle? 1 Samuel 2

The boy Samuel was taken to Shiloh and dedicated to the service of God. He was trained by the High Priest, Eli, and slept in the Tabernacle. Every year his mother made him a little cloak and took it to him when she and her husband went to Shiloh for the annual sacrifice. Eli blessed them and said, "May the Lord grant you other children in place of this one, for whom you asked." As is often the way, Hannah, having waited so long for a child, had more after Samuel—three sons and two daughters.

 Who called to Samuel in the night? 1 Samuel 3

When Samuel was a boy in Shiloh, the holy place had fallen into disrepute. Eli had grown very old, was almost blind, and his sons were the priests in charge. They had no love or respect for God and encouraged bad habits.

One night, not long before dawn, Samuel heard someone calling his name as he slept in the Tabernacle near the Ark. He ran to Eli and asked him what he wanted. "I did not call you," Eli replied. Samuel went to lie down, but again he heard a voice calling him. This happened three times, but the third time, Eli realized that God was calling Samuel. He told the boy that if he heard his name called again, he should reply, "Speak, Lord, thy servant hears thee."

Samuel did as he was told, and God told him that Eli's family, who were responsible for the disgrace of the shrine in Shiloh, were doomed.

This was the first time God spoke through Samuel. But by the time he grew up, all Israel recognized him as a Prophet of God.

 How did the Philistines capture the Ark of the Covenant? 1 Samuel 4

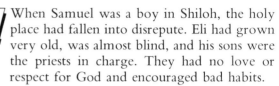 The First Book of Samuel tells the story of the continuing struggle between the Israelites and the Philistines, already familiar from the Book of Judges. The story of how the Ark was lost reflects God's disgust with the happenings at Shiloh.

There was a great battle where the Philistines out-fought the Israelites and caused many deaths. The Israelites then decided to take the Ark from Shiloh on to the battlefield with them, so that it could protect them. When the Philistines saw that the Israelites had brought the Ark of the Covenant on to the battlefield, they were afraid, saying, "They have brought their god with them!" They had heard what this god had done to the Egyptians. (In a way the Ark *did* represent the presence of Yahweh for the Israelites, and that was why they had brought it.)

Imagine the Philistines' surprise when they found, during the course of the battle, that they swept the Israelites from the field and captured the Ark. Among the Israelites killed were the evil sons of Eli, who himself died after hearing the news of the capture of the Ark.

Who was Dagon?

When the Philistine captured the Ark, they took it to Ashdod, which was probably the chief Philistine city at that time. They carried the Ark into the temple of Dagon, and set it by the image of Dagon himself. This Dagon was more or less the same kind of god as Baal, a god of the corn and harvest, and is said to have had the body and tail of a fish, though there is no real evidence for this. He was probably a god of the Canaanites, taken over by the Philistines when they settled in Canaan. When the people of Ashdod went into the temple next morning, they found the statue of Dagon had fallen face down in front of the Ark. They put it back in place, but next morning it was down again, and this time it was broken.

The fish-like tail of the Philistine god, Dagon, may have something to do with the former sea-going tradition of the Philistines.

How did the Ark return to Israel?
1 Samuel 5–6

The Philistines soon came to regret that they had captured the Ark of the Covenant. Not only did it result in the fall and breakage of the statue of their god Dagon, but the city of Ashdod was also afflicted with an epidemic. The Bible says the people were plagued with tumors, and their territory was overrun by rats. This sounds very like bubonic plague, which is carried by the fleas on rats (though, of course, no one knew that then).

When the Philistines took the Ark to Gath, which was another of their cities, the same disease broke out there. And the same thing happened at a third city, Ekron, where the people were not at all happy to receive the Ark, having heard of what had happened in Ashdod and Gath.

In the end, the Philistines wisely decided to send the Ark back to Israel, along with offerings which included five gold rats. The Ark arrived at a farm in Beth-shemesh, and the epidemic soon broke out there, killing 70 people. However, that seems to have been the end of it.

Then the Ark was taken to a nearby city and remained there, until it was taken to Jerusalem by King David.

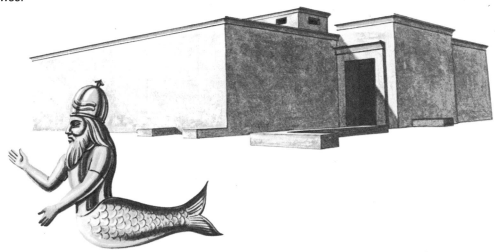

Why did the Israelites want a king?

When Samuel was in his prime, as Judge of all Israel, things improved. Once more, Israel turned towards God—that is, the true God, not the Canaanite gods like Baal. However, when he grew old, Samuel appointed his sons as Judges and, as had happened with Eli in an earlier time, the sons were not the equal of the father.

Meanwhile, the Israelites had still not got the better of the Philistines. The poor behavior of Samuel's sons and the need for strong military leadership persuaded the Elders of Israel that they should have a monarch—a king to rule over them and lead them in battle. In those days, most other nations had a king.

Samuel, naturally enough, thought this was a bad idea. He pointed out the disadvantages: a king would take men for his army, women for his servants, many people to plow his fields and grow his crops. He would take the best of their land, he would make them pay heavy taxes, and in the end, he would make them slaves.

Still the people persisted. They wanted a king to rule them and lead them into battle. So God told Samuel that if the people wanted a king, they should have one.

How was Saul chosen as king?
1 Samuel 9

Saul was the son of a man of the tribe of Benjamin. One day he set off looking for his father's donkeys, which had strayed. During that search, he happened to meet Samuel, whom (it seems) he had never heard of before. Advised by God, Samuel knew Saul was the man destined to be king of Israel.

The First Book of Samuel is difficult to follow sometimes because it consists of the work of more than one writer. In this section, a new writer seems to have taken over, one who was not opposed to the idea of monarchy but was in favor of a patriotic movement among the Israelites. It is probably significant that Saul came from the tribe of Benjamin, which was centrally placed and exposed to Philistine attacks. It was therefore likely to be the center of any movement designed to rally the disunited Israelites.

Why did Samuel anoint Saul?
1 Samuel 10

The Bible says that Samuel took a flask of oil and poured it over Saul's head. The act of anointing with oil was an official, religious act of consecration. Prophets and priests as well as kings were anointed. Quite how this ceremony began no one can say, but the act of pouring oil on the head of a king or priest symbolized the blessing that (it was hoped) he would "pour" on the people, through the grace of God.

What happened at Gilead? 1 Samuel 11

Saul was astonished when Samuel first told him what he was to become, and even after he had been accepted by most, though not all, of the Israelites as their king, he went back to work on his farm, plowing with his oxen.

What really established him as king of a nation that became more thoroughly united than it had been since the days of Joshua was the battle at Gilead.

The city of Gilead was besieged by the Ammonites. The people had no hope of help from the rest of Israel and promised to surrender if none arrived within a week. The Ammonites allowed the messengers asking for help to leave the city, sure that no Israelites would help them. When Saul heard this, he became angry. He killed two of his oxen, chopped them up and sent pieces to every tribe in Israel saying that those who did not obey his summons to fight would have their own oxen treated in the same way.

The result was that he raised the biggest army Israel had seen in over 200 years, and the Ammonites were defeated.

Who were the Ammonites?

The Ammonites, who were so resoundingly defeated by Saul in his first battle as king of Israel, were old enemies of Israel. Their country was in what is now the kingdom of Jordan, and according to Hebrew tradition, they were descended from Lot, Abraham's nephew. Their name lives on in the name of the present capital of Jordan, Amman.

Q What animals were kept by the Israelites?

A In the days of the monarchy, farming changed a little. There were more and bigger farms, although most were still very small. Nevertheless, the farmer's life was now less simple. A greater variety of animals was kept, although the main flocks were still sheep and goats. There were probably more chickens and more oxen than in the days before the settlement in Palestine.

A great number of animals were sacrificed as burnt offerings, but only certain animals were "clean"—or, to use the later Hebrew word, *kosher*—which meant "fit for sacrifice." Both camels and pigs were excluded from this category, and therefore, they were not kept by religious people.

A shepherd and his flock. This relationship was often seen by Biblical writers as a mirror of the relationship between God and his people.

Q What is a goad?

A A goad is a wooden pole, up to 3 feet (0.90 m) long, with a spike at one end. A farmer, when plowing, held the plow steady with one hand and held a goad with the other, to prick the oxen and urge them on. In the Book of Judges, there is a reference to a great Hebrew warrior killing vast numbers of the enemy with his ox goad. At that time, the metal tips at the end of goads were supplied by the Philistines, who held the monopoly on metalworking.

Goads are sometimes mentioned in the Bible in a metaphorical sense. Good advice, for instance, is said to be a goad to good behavior.

Q Why did Samuel turn against Saul?
1 Samuel 13–15

A After his first great victory against the Philistines at Gilead, Saul's generalship was less successful. Although the whole of Israel rallied to Saul, the Philistines gathered an even greater army. Samuel failed to arrive to offer a sacrifice to God, and Saul's soldiers began to drift away. In the end, losing patience, Saul made the sacrifice himself, although it was strictly a task that only a priest should undertake. When Samuel did arrive, just as Saul had finished, he was angry. He told Saul that God would take the kingdom from him and give it to another, who was already chosen. (This was a reference to David.)

It is hard not to feel sorry for King Saul. After all, he had not wanted to be king in the first place. Samuel's behavior toward him was very changeable, to say the least, and it is difficult to follow the logic of it. This is the result of the Books of Samuel being compiled from more than one account, whose different authors do not have the same opinions or beliefs.

Who tore Samuel's robe? 1 Samuel 15

Having defeated numerous other enemies, Saul prepared to attack the Amalekites, the nomadic bandits who were among Israel's oldest enemies. Samuel brought instructions from God that the Amalekites were to be utterly destroyed. This order was carried out, but incompletely. The king of the Amalekites was captured alive, and the best of their flocks of animals were preserved—ordinary Israelites saw no point in killing them.

Samuel reprimanded Saul in fierce terms, and when Saul asked forgiveness, he refused it. As he turned to go, Saul in desperation grabbed Samuel's robe, tearing it. Samuel remarked that the kingdom would be torn from Saul just as Saul had torn the robe.

There are several versions of the quarrel between Samuel and Saul in the Bible. Probably the main trouble was a contest for authority between the Prophet (Samuel) and the King (Saul).

Boys started work, keeping an eye on the flocks, at a very early age.

What was the ceremony of purification?

God sent Samuel to Bethlehem to anoint a new king of Israel whom he was to find among the sons of Jesse. Fearful of Saul's reaction if he learned the purpose of the visit, Samuel said he was going to sacrifice to God, and he told the people of Bethlehem to purify themselves for a festival.

The ancient Hebrews had strong ideas on what was "clean" and "unclean." For example, some animals were "unclean" and not to be eaten. They regarded sin as a kind of moral dirtiness, from which people had to be cleaned, or purified. Special rites of purification were laid down in the Law for almost any situation, such as how to cleanse a place where a murder had been committed, or where a leper had been.

Why was Jesse's youngest son not at home when Samuel came? 1 Samuel 16

When Samuel arrived in Bethlehem, he asked Jesse to come to the feast and to bring his sons, whom he would purify before the sacrifice. The reason Samuel wanted to see the sons of Jesse was that, among them, he knew, was the future king of Israel.

The first son, Eliab, was such a splendid specimen of a young man that Samuel thought

he must be the one. Then he remembered that Saul too had been a splendid young giant of a man, and that a man is judged not by his appearance but by his heart.

Six more sons came forward, but Samuel knew that none of them was God's choice. He asked Jesse if all his sons were present. Jesse answered that the youngest, David, was not there because he was away looking after the sheep. "Send and fetch him," said Samuel. "We shall not sit down to the feast until he arrives."

As soon as Samuel saw David, he knew that he was the one God had chosen to succeed Saul. Samuel anointed David, who felt filled with the Spirit of God, and that never left him.

Q What does "gird up your loins" mean?

A Clothes were simple in Biblical times. The most common article of dress, worn by both men and women, was a kind of simple shift or tunic, reaching to the knees and gathered in at the waist by a belt, or girdle, which was itself simply another strip of cloth. Such a garment, like the belted plaid worn by the Highlanders of Scotland, was not very convenient when you were going to do anything energetic, such as fighting a battle. It was then necessary to "gird up your loins," or tuck the hem of the tunic into the girdle. The same thing applied if you were wearing a simple loincloth, as ordinary workers did.

The expression was sometimes used in a metaphorical way, much as we should say, "Pull your socks up!"

Q How did David enter Saul's household? 1 Samuel 16

A It seems clear from the stories of Saul in the Bible that his mental state was slightly unbalanced, probably as a result of the problems he was faced with as king. In particular, he seems to have been what today would be called a manic-depressive, meaning that at times he was very low and depressed and at other times he was the opposite—wildly elated. The Spirit of God had departed from him.

Saul's servants had the good idea of getting someone to play music to Saul when he was suffering from what they called an evil spirit. Saul agreed, and when one of his servants said he had seen the youngest son of Jesse play very beautifully on the harp, Saul summoned him. Thus David came into the king's household.

The harp that David played was probably something like this instrument, which is in an Israeli museum. There are 11 strings across a sounding board, decorated with mosaics.

Q What did people drink in Biblical times?

A Even water was something of a luxury in ancient Palestine. In times of drought, it could only be bought from traveling watersellers. Otherwise, it had to be fetched from the local well, though some households might have their own supply.

People also drank goats' milk, and perhaps sheep's milk occasionally, both probably in a sour, fermented form, something like yogurt. They were, of course, very fond of wine. There are a great many references to wine—growing and making it, drinking too much of it and so on— in the Bible.

Other Middle Eastern peoples also drank beer, but we do not hear of the Israelites making or drinking beer.

What was the challenge of Goliath? 1 Samuel 17

 Neither the Israelites nor their enemies the Philistines (or other hostile neighbors) had professional armies. The warriors of King Saul were also ordinary farmers. However, there were a few specialists: famous warriors, successful generals (like King David's general, Joab later), and champions, like Goliath of Gath.

Goliath was a giant, though perhaps not quite as big as the 10 feet (3 m) tall that the Bible says he was. He wore bronze armor, which would have been rare then, certainly among the Israelites.

Goliath challenged the Israelites to produce a champion of their own. The two would fight, and if the Israelite champion won, the Philistines would surrender; if Goliath won, the Israelites would surrender. This form of single combat avoided the need for a lot of family men and farmers to be needlessly killed.

David went to the Israelites' camp and accepted Goliath's challenge, rejecting Saul's offer of his own armor.

 ## Where was Gath?

 Gath was one of the five chief city-states of the Philistines, and the one nearest to the territory of the Israelites. It was therefore often involved in military conflicts, and was later captured by King David during his wars against the Philistines. Gath had a reputation for producing very large men, so, not surprisingly, it was the home town of Goliath.

After David's time, Gath lost its importance, probably as the result of frequent damage in war—it was also sacked by Uzziah, king of Judah, in the 8th century BC. As a result, we no longer know exactly where it was.

What weapon did David take to use against Goliath?

The Bible tells us in detail about the weapons and armor of Goliath. It even tells us the weight of the metal head of his spear. Besides the spear, which was as big as a weaver's beam, he also carried a sword. Against this bronze-armored giant came David the shepherd boy, carrying nothing but a leather sling and five white pebbles. The story is like one of those Jack-the-Giantkiller fairy stories, and there is equally little doubt who will win. Goliath never had a chance!

A round stone propelled by a sling could reach great speeds and be amazingly accurate. It was the chief weapon of the shepherd boys against marauding animals, and they spent many, many hours practicing with it. Goliath, with his vast spear (which was not good for throwing) and bronze sword, was at a great disadvantage against an opponent who could fling a bullet-like stone at his forehead from quite a distance.

 ## How did Saul greet David's victory?

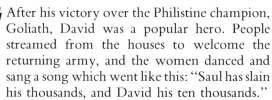 After his victory over the Philistine champion, Goliath, David was a popular hero. People streamed from the houses to welcome the returning army, and the women danced and sang a song which went like this: "Saul has slain his thousands, and David his ten thousands."

Not surprisingly, Saul was very annoyed that David's exploits should be considered greater than his, and from that time, he became jealous and suspicious of David.

Q Who were Michal and Jonathan?

A They were the daughter and one of the sons of King Saul. Jonathan became David's close friend, and Michal became his wife—the reward, as in lots of fairy tales, of the young champion who killed the wicked giant. After the break between Saul and David, Michal had saved David from her father's jealousy, with the result that she was given to another husband (women had few rights in those days). After Saul's death, David took her back. This was possibly a way of making his claim to the kingship more secure, but it seems that there was genuine love between the two. However, there were no children of the marriage, and we hear little more of Michal.

Jonathan is something of a hero in the First Book of Samuel, second only to David himself, although in general the writer is not at all friendly to Saul's family. If Jonathan had not been killed, he and David would presumably have become rivals for the throne.

David and Goliath.

What was Jonathan's secret message to David? 1 Samuel 20

Because of Saul's hostility, David was forced to flee from the royal household and hide in the countryside. He managed to get a message to Jonathan asking why Saul should want to kill him. Jonathan replied that Saul could not want to kill him, because he would have said so. But David was unwilling to risk returning to Saul's household, and he arranged that Jonathan should send him a message to let him know if Saul was angry with him or not. He was to hide somewhere in sight of the place where Jonathan went to practice shooting with his bow and arrows. If he fired three arrows on one side of the target, it meant David was safe. If he fired them on the other side, it meant he was in danger.

Jonathan found that it was true—Saul did wish to kill David. He went into the fields as they had arranged and fired the arrows to the side meaning danger! He and David said farewell, and David fled to Nob.

Why was Ahimelech killed?
1 Samuel 21–2

As a refugee from Saul's murderous jealousy, David made his way to the city of Nob (no one now knows where it was), where he was kindly received by the priest, Ahimelech. But Ahim-

elech was surprised that David came alone. David told him he was on a secret mission, and the priest gave him some of the holy bread, which was the only food available. After gaining possession of Goliath's sword, which was kept there, David left rather hurriedly.

Unfortunately, one of Saul's men, named Doeg, had seen David at Nob, and he told Saul how he had seen David and Ahimelech together. Saul was convinced that they were plotting against him. He gave orders that Ahimelech and his family, and all the other priests of Nob, should be killed. His men were unwilling to obey, but Doeg himself did the job, killing men, women and children with his own hand. One of Ahimelech's sons, Abiathar, escaped and joined David.

What happened in the Cave of Adullam? 1 Samuel 22

From Nob, David fled to Gath, and from there to Adullam, where he took refuge in a cave. His brothers and other members of his family joined him there, and so did many others—mostly people in some kind of trouble. Soon he had a band of about 400.

Saul too sheltered in a cave when he was following David.
David found him asleep, but spared his life (1 Samuel 24).

The Philistines were attacking the town of Keilah, not far away, and David asked God whether he should go and fight them. God said he should, but his companions felt they had enough troubles already without making war on the Philistines. But God promised a victory, and David set off to Keilah with his discontented band, who nevertheless inflicted a defeat on the Philistines as God had promised.

Groups of discontented people are still sometimes called "Adullamites." For example, in the 19th century in Britain, the name was given to a group of Members of Parliament who were dissatisfied with their party's policy.

 How did Abigail save her husband? 1 Samuel 25

 When David was living as an outlaw, with a band now of 600 to feed, he sent messengers to a rich man called Nabal who lived at Carmel. This man's flocks and other possessions had not been harmed by David's men, and now they asked for a contribution. Nabal, whose name means "stupid," was a mean and surly fellow, and gave them a rude answer.

When David heard this, he was furious. He

Abigail's combination of a generous gift of food, plus female charm, prevented the destruction of her household.

ordered 400 of his men to arm themselves, and they set off for Carmel with the intention of destroying Nabal and all his family. But Nabal had a very sensible wife, Abigail, who hastily gathered a large "present"—200 loaves, five sheep ready for roasting and other food. She spoke so charmingly to David that she won him over completely.

Not long after this, Nabal died of a stroke. David suggested to Abigail that she become his wife, and she accepted.

A water flask and spear head of the kind David would have carried.

Saul and the Witch of Endor

Q **Why did Saul visit the Witch of Endor?** 1 Samuel 28

A Before the fatal battle of Gilboa, Saul, as he looked across at the Philistines' force, was afraid. He could seek no comfort or advice from Samuel because he had died some time before, and when he tried to communicate with God, there was no answer. But such was his need for hope and guidance that he instructed his men to find a woman with second sight—a witch—and one of them said there was such a woman at Endor.

Witchcraft, and all forms of magic, were, of course, considered evil by the Israelites, and Saul himself is said to have banished from the land all those who had dealings with ghosts or spirits. That he should seek guidance from such a person himself showed how desperate he was —and also that he had indeed lost the favor of the Lord.

Q **What was Saul told by the spirit of Samuel?**

A Saul went to the Witch of Endor in disguise. When he asked her to tell his fortune, she was suspicious because all dealings with magic were illegal. But Saul eventually persuaded her that no harm would come to her, and at his request, she called up the spirit of Samuel.

Samuel was not pleased to be disturbed in this way, but Saul told him about the trouble he was in—besieged by the Philistines and forsaken by God. What should he do?

Samuel had little sympathy and no comfort. "God has done what he foretold through me," he said, meaning that Saul would lose the kingdom. In the forthcoming battle, Samuel said, "God will give the victory to the Philistines."

Q **When did David march with the Philistines?**

A David had realized that, one day, he was likely to be killed by Saul, and so he decided to take refuge in the territory of the Philistines. He went to Gath, where he was well received by the king, Achish, who gave him land where his band of 600 men could live. They kept themselves occupied fighting the Amalekites and other enemies. However, when the Philistines mustered for a great campaign against Saul and the Israelites, Achish asked David to take the field with him. David promised he would.

However, the other Philistine leaders objected to the presence of Hebrews in their army, believing that it was unwise to trust them, whatever Achish said: they might change sides in the middle of the battle. Achish therefore sent David and his men home again, and David was saved from having to take part in a battle against his own people.

Who died on Mount Gilboa?
1 Samuel 31

On Mount Gilboa the Israelites were routed by the Philistines, as God had forewarned. Saul's three oldest sons, including Jonathan, were killed, and Saul himself was badly wounded. Rather than fall into the hands of the pursuing Philistines, Saul told his armor-bearer (a position once held by David) to kill him with his sword, but the man could not bring himself to do it. So Saul took the sword and stabbed himself to death.

Did the Israelites fight with chariots?

A chariot was a two-wheeled vehicle, pulled by a horse or a pair of horses, and carrying at least two men—the driver and an archer. Often there was a third man. Chariots were in use in the Middle East from an early date. We know, for example, that the Egyptian army that pursued the Israelites when they left Egypt had chariots, and they had been used in Mesopotamia even earlier, perhaps before 2500 BC.

War chariots were also used on the plains of Palestine by the Canaanites when the Israelites entered the country, but except for ceremonial parades, they do not seem to have been employed by the Israelites themselves until the time of David.

What happened after Saul's death?

David had been anointed many years before by Samuel, but the old Prophet died before Saul. Saul's grown-up sons died in battle against the Philistines along with him, so Saul left no direct adult heir. All the same, David did not succeed to the kingship easily.

He was acknowledged as king by Judah, his own tribe, but Abner, Saul's old general, remained loyal to Saul's family. He proclaimed Isbosheth, a younger son of Saul, as king of the other 11 tribes. The result was civil war.

David's forces, commanded by Joab, won the first battle, but the decisive event was a quarrel between Abner and Isbosheth, which resulted in Abner changing sides. Abner was later killed by Joab in a private quarrel, but soon afterward Isbosheth was murdered by two of his own officers. After that, David had no rivals, and his reign—an heroic period in the history of Israel—began.

An Egyptian chariot—the "tank" of ancient warfare

How long did the monarchy last?

The Israelites adopted the idea of monarchy because they needed a strong ruler to unite them against the Philistines, and because other, neighboring peoples had monarchs. Saul, the first monarch, became king some time about 1050 BC. He was succeeded by David, and David was succeeded by Solomon, who died about 922 BC. After that, the kingdom split into two—Israel and Judah. The kingdom of Judah survived until the Babylonian Exile in the 6th century BC.

What were the weapons of King David's army?

A heavily armed Israelite warrior carried a spear, with a metal tip on a wooden shaft, and a sword or dagger. Swords are mentioned as early as Joshua, but they were not in common use until much later.

More lightly armed soldiers carried slings—the weapon that David had used to defeat Goliath—and probably bows and arrows. The latter were probably the most effective weapons. They were a very early human invention, which had been in use in Mesopotamia well over 1,000 years before David's time.

Did David's army have cavalry?

Horses were used by Middle Eastern peoples well before the Israelites settled in Canaan. During the flight from Egypt, the Israelites had been pursued by horse-drawn chariots, and their conquest of Canaan was made more difficult by the presence of these among the defenses of some of the Canaanite cities.

The Israelites had few dealings with horses until the time of the monarchy. David captured many horses and chariots in warfare, and the larger army of Solomon included thousands of horse-drawn chariots. Solomon also engaged in a complicated trade in horses, buying them in the north and selling them in Egypt. At Megiddo, archeologists have found what may be the remains of stables dating from Solomon's time, which had room for many

horses. Cavalry—that is, soldiers on horseback—was unknown in the Middle East then, although there were nomadic, mounted bowmen among northern peoples in Asia.

Did David's soldiers wear armor?

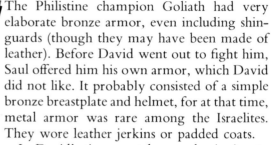

The Philistine champion Goliath had very elaborate bronze armor, even including shinguards (though they may have been made of leather). Before David went out to fight him, Saul offered him his own armor, which David did not like. It probably consisted of a simple bronze breastplate and helmet, for at that time, metal armor was rare among the Israelites. They wore leather jerkins or padded coats.

In David's time, metals were beginning to become more common. Then Israelite warriors might wear a metal (probably bronze or copper) helmet and carry a metal shield.

Where is the City of David?

This was the name given to Jerusalem by David himself, who captured it from the Jebusites and made it his capital. Because of its central position and its good defensive location, it made a good capital for the united kingdom of Israel, and later the kingdom of Judah. It also stood among many sacred sites and so was equally suited as a religious capital, which it became—first, when the Ark was transferred there and, later, when the Temple was built.

Today, the name "City of David" is given to the oldest part of Jerusalem, south of the Temple area. Jerusalem was, however, already an old city in David's time, having been inhabited then for at least 1,000 years.

Bethlehem is also sometimes called the "City of David," because it was there that David grew up.

When did the Ark of the Covenant come to Jerusalem? 2 Samuel 5

After becoming the acknowledged king of a united country, David attacked the Jebusites, whose city was Jerusalem. They were a

Canaanite mountain people of mixed origin, and they had been in conflict with the Israelites before. Joshua had killed their king in battle, but had not taken the city, which was then called Jebus. Some time later, we hear of the city being set on fire by the men of Judah. But the Jebusites held out until David's general, Joab, captured it by reaching the heart of the city via the main water-course cut in the rock.

David made Jerusalem his capital, and had the Ark of the Covenant, containing the stone tablets engraved with the Law of Moses, brought there. The royal palace and the Temple were not built until the reign of Solomon.

Q How did David meet Bathsheba?
2 Samuel 11

A In ancient Palestine nearly 3,000 years ago, a man might have more than one wife; King David had several. But it was, of course, a great sin for a man to take another man's wife. This, nevertheless, is what David did.

Bathsheba was married to Uriah, an officer in David's army. It was by chance that David saw her, bathing in the courtyard of her house. He saw her from the roof of his palace, and was struck by her beauty. He summoned her to the palace, and soon they began a love affair.

Q Who were the Hittites?

A The Israelites were people with the blood of many races in their veins. David himself was partly of Moabite descent, for example, and Uriah, the husband of Bathsheba and an officer in David's army, was a Hittite.

The Hittites were established in what is now Turkey. We know a good deal about them through the finds of archeologists, for they were at one time a very powerful people, almost the equal of the empires of Egypt and Mesopotamia. By David's time, however, their great days of empire were over. There were still some Hittites living in Palestine, where Hittite colonies had been established, but most of them lived farther north. Not long after this time, the Hittites disappear from history.

Q How did Uriah die? 2 Samuel 11

A God had promised that he would never withdraw his favor from David as he had from Saul. Yet David was an ordinary man, not without sin, and perhaps his worst act was his attempt to conceal his affair with Bathsheba.

David sent secret orders (which were carried by Uriah himself) to his general Joab, who was besieging Rabbah, a city of the Ammonites. In those orders, he told Joab to place Uriah where he knew the fighting would be fiercest and to give him no reinforcements if he came under attack. As a result, Uriah was killed. Bathsheba mourned for him, but when the mourning period was over, David sent for her, and she became his wife.

A reconstruction of the water tunnel used by David's forces to give access to Jerusalem. The tunnel begins behind the city walls and leads to the spring (1). The tunnel could be closed by stones (2) so no enemy could use it.

What was the story that Nathan told David? 2 Samuel 12

After Uriah's death, David married Bathsheba, and in time, she had a son. David's crime in taking Bathsheba and arranging the death of her husband seemed to be forgotten. Then Nathan the Prophet arrived at David's court and told him the story of the rich man with large flocks and the poor man who had but one little lamb, which he cared for so much that she was almost like a daughter instead of a pet. One day a traveler stopped at the rich man's house, and the latter, too mean to use one of his own animals, took the poor man's lamb and served it up for dinner.

When David heard the story, he was full of righteous anger. "The man deserved to die," he said. "Who was he?" "You are the man," Nathan told him.

David was guilty of murder in sending Uriah to certain death, but he was later punished when his own son died.

Who was David's eldest son?

David's first wife, Michal, daughter of Saul, had no children. His first son was the child of Bathsheba, and when Nathan accused David of murdering Uriah and stealing his wife, he warned him that as punishment for his sin, though he would not die himself, the child would die.

Soon afterwards, the boy became ill. David prayed and fasted, and even refused to go to bed, but after seven days, the boy died.

Later, Bathsheba had another son. This was Solomon, who was to succeed David as king of Israel.

How was Nathan's prophecy fulfilled?

Nathan had warned David that, for his sin in stealing Uriah's wife and causing his death, his eldest son should die. He prophesied also that his family would henceforth be constantly warring against each other. This explained the subsequent troubles in the royal family, which were inevitable when a man had as many wives and children as David had. These were very bitter times for the king. Among other dreadful deeds, one son, Amnon, was killed by his half-brother, Absalom.

Who was Ahithophel?

The most serious of the family troubles that King David had to deal with was the rebellion of his son, Absalom. What made it especially serious was that the rebels were joined by Ahithophel.

Ahithophel is described as David's counselor. He was clearly a very intelligent man, who joined Absalom because he thought the rebellion was likely to be successful—as it might have been if Absalom had followed Ahithophel's advice. As it was, David was forced to flee from Jerusalem, which was occupied by Absalom's forces. Ahithophel advised Absalom to send him at the head of a powerful force to catch David and kill him while he was on the run. Absalom rejected this plan, and Ahithopel realized then that the rebellion would not succeed. So he left Absalom, returned to his house, put his affairs in order, and killed himself.

What happened to Absalom?

As Ahithophel had realized, it was essential to catch the king quickly if Absalom's rebellion were to succeed. Once David had time to organize his forces, it was doomed.

The battle between the two armies—Absalom and the men of Israel, David and the men of Judah—took place in wooded country. During the battle, as he rode under a tree, Absalom's hair was caught in the branches (he was well known for the length and thickness of his hair). David had given orders that his son's life was to be spared at all costs, but when the tough old general, Joab, heard that the rebellious prince was strung up helpless in the forest, he rode there at once and killed him.

David had not taken part in the battle because his soldiers had persuaded him not to—if they lost, he would still be able to fight again. When news came that his forces had been successful against the rebels, he was overjoyed. But when a second messenger brought the news that Absalom was dead, David was filled with grief. He shut himself away to mourn in private, until Joab roused him out of it with his just complaint that David acted as if he would have preferred all those loyal to him to have died instead of the leader of his enemies.

The traditional Tomb of Absalom, in the Kidron valley in Jerusalem.

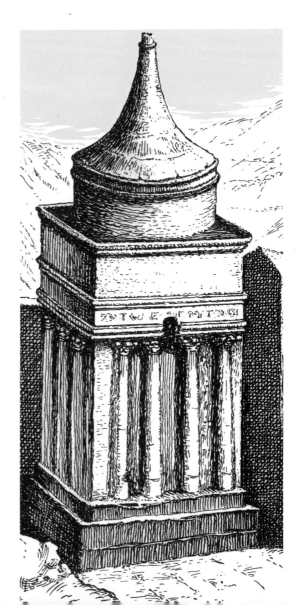

Did the Israelites use mules?

In King David's time, chariots, drawn by horses, were just coming into use (other people had employed them much earlier), but cavalry was still unknown. The animal that was usually ridden was a donkey; even a king would ride one without anyone thinking it undignified. However, the animal Absalom was mounted on in the forest of Ephron when his hair got caught in a tree, was a mule.

It is only in David's time that we hear of mules being ridden, though there are several references to them after that. Mules are the offspring of cross-breeding a horse and a donkey. They cannot breed themselves. Cross-breeding was against the religious law of the Israelites, so David's people must have got their mules through trade with others.

Who succeeded David as king?

When King David was an old man, he made it known that he wished his son Solomon to succeed him. Solomon's mother was Bathsheba, undoubtedly David's favorite wife, but he was not the oldest son.

That was his half-brother, Adonijah, who plotted to seize the throne while David was still alive. The plot failed, and David had Solomon anointed as king by Zadok the priest, with the support of Nathan the Prophet. Although Adonijah's life was spared, when Solomon was safely established as king after David's death, Solomon feared that Adonijah still had ambitions for power; he therefore had him killed.

What are the Psalms?

The Psalms are religious Hebrew songs, or poems, or hymns. The singing of Psalms was very popular, and probably began within a century or two of the conquest of Canaan. The Israelites would have known many Psalms by heart.

We do not know who wrote the Psalms. According to tradition, they are largely the work of King David, famous as a poet and musician. He may well have written some of them (especially Psalms 18, 29, 88, and 89), but

some were obviously written later. For example, the Temple is mentioned in several Psalms, but it was not built in David's time. Others also show signs of being composed much later, though in some cases it is possible that David was the original author and that his words were revised by later scribes.

What does "Alleluia" mean?

When Psalms were sung in Old Testament times, there was a great deal of excitement, with dancing, shouting and chanting, something like the hymn-singing in the most lively Evangelical churches of today. Often, Psalms were sung by two choirs—for example, one representing Earth and the other Heaven. There would be a certain competition between them, and the cries of "Alleluia" or "Hallelujah!" which is usually translated "Praise the Lord!"—really meant "*You* praise the Lord!"—an invitation to the other choir to show what they could do.

What was the population of Israel?

The Israelites under King Solomon probably numbered about 1 million. However, the total population of the united kingdoms of Israel and Judah would have been more than that because many Canaanites and other peoples still lived there. There are signs, such as the amount of building, that the population was growing during the reign of Solomon; this may also have been true in the preceding reign, despite David's many wars.

What was God's gift to Solomon?
1 Kings 3

Solomon went to Gibeon to offer sacrifice at the hill shrine there, and that night God appeared to him in a dream. God asked Solomon what gift he would like, and Solomon asked for "a heart with skill to listen," so that he would be a good judge among his people. God was very pleased with this reply—after all, Solomon might have asked for long life and good health for himself—so he granted that gift and added more, which Solomon had not asked for. He would have great wealth and honor, more than any other king, and if he obeyed God's law, he would also have long life.

Was there a queen of Israel?

The original purpose of a monarch was to lead his people in war. In those days it was thought that only a man could do this. In any case, the Israelites generally considered women to be inferior to men, although individual women sometimes had great influence, and women in general were better protected in Israel than in many other societies of that time.

It was not forbidden for a man, and especially a king, to have more than one wife (Solomon had dozens), so there was usually no particular queen, though a favorite wife, like David's Bathsheba, might in practice hold that position. In later years, however, the position changed in favor of a single wife, or queen.

In general, there were no ruling "queens" of Israel (in the way that there were queens of, for example, Egypt). But, as always, there were exceptions, such as Queen Athaliah. She seized control of the government of Judah after her son was killed in 842 BC and reigned for about five years.

What was the Judgement of Solomon? 1 Kings 3

The main job of the king, when he was not leading his army in war, was to be a judge, resolving difficult disputes among his people. David had been a mighty warrior. His son Solomon was a great judge, renowned for his wisdom.

The most famous example of Solomon's wise judgment is the case of the baby claimed by two mothers. Neither of the women had a husband; they shared a house and both had had a baby about the same time, but one baby had died and both claimed the survivor.

After listening to their arguments for a long while, Solomon sent for a sword. The only way to decide the matter, he said, was to cut the baby in half and give one half to each woman.

At once, one of the women begged him to do no such thing, but rather give the baby to the other woman. Solomon judged that she was the mother, because she would rather lose her baby to another woman than see it killed.

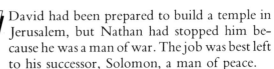

When was the Temple built?
1 Kings 5–7

David had been prepared to build a temple in Jerusalem, but Nathan had stopped him because he was a man of war. The job was best left to his successor, Solomon, a man of peace.

Although the building of the Temple was certainly a great task, it was not a large building. It was simply a more permanent form of the Tabernacle and was about $88\frac{1}{2}$ feet (27 m) long, $29\frac{1}{2}$ feet (9 m) wide and 44 feet (13.5 m) high. However, unlike a Christian church or a Jewish synagogue, it was not intended to admit worshipers.

The Temple was completed between the 4th and 11th years of Solomon's reign, probably between about 957 and 950 BC. Though small, it was beautiful, and it had been very expensive to build and decorate. However, there was plenty of money: David had left a good deal of treasure for the purpose.

Who were the laborers who built the Temple? 1 Kings 5–7

A great many men were involved in building the Temple in Jerusalem, even allowing for the exaggeration of numbers common in the Old Testament. According to the account in the Second Book of Kings, Solomon raised a labor force of 30,000 men to haul in the timber supplies. He had 80,000 quarrymen and 70,000 hauliers to deal with the stone, and these figures did not include the 3,300 foremen in charge of the work. Of course, not all these men would have been at work at the same time, since they were also family men and farmers, or had other jobs. Of those employed in transporting the timber, only one third of the men worked at any one time.

Solomon was also engaged on other building projects, besides the Temple itself. One of these was the Hall of Judgment.

Where did the best timber come from?

All the early civilizations of the Middle East were short of timber, and imported it from the forests of Lebanon. The cedars of Lebanon are often mentioned in the Bible, and they provided the timber for Solomon's temple. There are still a few stands of these slow-growing trees in Lebanon, but in Old Testament times, the forests must have been huge.

The timber was cut by the men of King Hiram of Tyre, floated down the Mediterranean coast to the harbor at what is now Jaffa, and dragged overland (and uphill!) for about 15½ miles (25 km) to Jerusalem.

Where did Solomon hire craftsmen to build the Temple?

Solomon had plenty of unskilled laborers among his own people, and these were forced to work for a certain amount of time on his building projects. But he did not have many skilled builders and craftsmen. The stone-cutting was done by some of Solomon's people, some of King Hiram's and some Gebalites. These were men from Gebal, a Phoenician city which the Greeks called Byblos, and we can guess that they were the most skilled stone-cutters.

Much of the artistic metalwork was done by a man called Hiram, who came from the Phoenician city of Tyre although he was not related to its king, also called Hiram. His mother was an Israelite though his father had been a Phoenician from Tyre.

What did a cherub look like?

When we think of a cherub, we think of a fat boy baby with wings and no clothes. This is the picture we owe to artists since the European Renaissance of the 15th century, but it is nothing like the cherubim of the Old Testament. The cherubim that guarded the Ark of the Covenant in Solomon's Temple were rather fierce-looking winged creatures with lions' bodies and sphinxes' heads. They belong to a family of similar creatures which decorated the temples of other Middle Eastern peoples, such as the Hittites, the Babylonians and the Egyptians.

What was in the Temple?

Solomon's Temple was similar in plan to the temples of other Middle Eastern peoples in the 10th century BC. It was not a place of worship but a house for God. The invisible God was present in a special way in the Temple, and as a result, unlike the temples of other religions, Solomon's contained no image or statue.

The building was long and narrow. Two bronze columns, separate from the building itself, stood at the top of the flight of steps leading to the porch. Beyond were two chambers: the Holy Place and, at the far end, the Holy of Holies, in which was the Ark of the Covenant. This was guarded by two giant cherubim that were 15 feet (nearly 5 m) high.

There were probably other buildings around the Temple, which stood in a large courtyard. Worshipers came to the Temple, but only priests were allowed inside.

When was the harvest?

In Palestine, the main growing season was not the summer but the winter, when it was still warm, but wetter than the summer. The main harvest season was therefore spring and early summer (there is no real spring or autumn season). Barley was harvested in April and early May, while wheat, which ripened later, was harvested in May and early June. The harvest had to be completed quickly, before the hot, dry weather dried up the crops. The grain was cut by hand with sickles which, in the early days, had blades of flint, copper or bronze, but which, from the time of King David, were made of iron.

The end of the harvest was celebrated in the Feast of Weeks (Pentecost), and the Feast of Tabernacles.

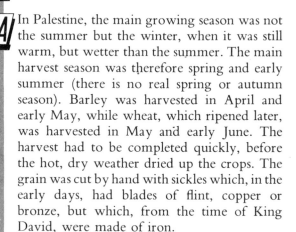

Harvesting the vines in the Jordan valley.

How did Solomon make Israel a richer country?

The victories of King David established the kingdom securely, and Solomon, his son and successor, reaped the benefits. As a consequence, he has been remembered throughout history not only for his wisdom but also for his wealth.

As king, Solomon controlled all the country's international trade, and this was the basis of his wealth. He traded to Ophir, in the Yemen, together with his ally, King Hiram of Tyre—who provided the ships and sailors. He probably had a trade treaty with the Queen of Sheba, who was sufficiently interested in the kingdom to pay a famous visit to Solomon. He also took advantage of the position of the country as a link between Egypt and Syria,

doing business with both countries.

General prosperity meant that the king also earned more from his royal estates, and from taxes, which were levied on trade (customs and excise) and on income (paid in kind, as a percentage of the crop). International developments favored Israel's prosperity in several ways, of which the most important was that, unusually for this period, peace prevailed in the region.

Where was the city of Megiddo?

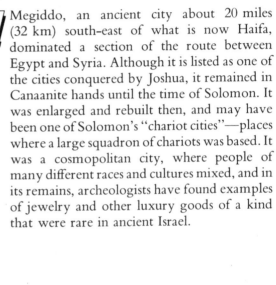

Megiddo, an ancient city about 20 miles (32 km) south-east of what is now Haifa, dominated a section of the route between Egypt and Syria. Although it is listed as one of the cities conquered by Joshua, it remained in Canaanite hands until the time of Solomon. It was enlarged and rebuilt then, and may have been one of Solomon's "chariot cities"—places where a large squadron of chariots was based. It was a cosmopolitan city, where people of many different races and cultures mixed, and in its remains, archeologists have found examples of jewelry and other luxury goods of a kind that were rare in ancient Israel.

Who was the Queen of Sheba?
1 Kings 10

Saba, or "Sheba" as it is called in the King James Bible, was a country in the south of Arabia, the region now known as the Yemen. The Sabaeans were rich merchants, operating both on the sea, where they almost rivaled the Phoenicians, and on land. The famous visit of the Queen of Sheba to King Solomon, which like many events of this period is described in both the Books of Kings and Chronicles, was probably connected with some commercial arrangement.

The Queen traveled overland in a great camel caravan, loaded with luxury goods. But she found Solomon's court even richer than her own, and became quite disheartened by all Solomon's wealth. After enjoying Solomon's lavish hospitality, she returned home, but there is a tradition that she became one of Solomon's wives and had a son by him. This son, Menelek,

is said to have settled in Ethiopia, where he became the founder of a royal house.

Why did God grow angry with Solomon? 1 Kings 11

Among Solomon's wives was a daughter of the Egyptian pharaoh, and she remained his favorite. He had a great many others, however—1,000 in all, including 700 who were important enough to be classed as princesses. Like his marriage to Pharaoh's daughter, many of these were "political" marriages to foreign princesses. The Bible mentions wives that were Moabite, Ammonite, Edomite, Sidonian and

Hittite. Solomon was, according to the Bible, devoted to all of them!

The Israelites were undecided about polygamy (having more than one wife). It was not forbidden to have many wives, if a man could afford it (and Solomon certainly could), but it was not considered desirable. It is obvious that people were moving toward a belief that one wife was enough, even for kings.

Solomon's trouble, however, arose because so many of his wives were foreign. God had warned against marrying foreign wives because they would tempt a man to worship their gods, and this was what Solomon had done—although probably only as a political gesture. It was for this reason that God told Solomon that his son would lose all but one tribe—the end of the unified kingdom.

Q Who was Jeroboam? 1 Kings 11

A Jeroboam was the leader of a rebellion against Solomon. The Bible tells us that he was one of Solomon's courtiers, a young man with plenty of energy who impressed Solomon so much that he gave him an important job in charge of the labor gangs. Advised by the Prophet Ahijah that he would become king of Israel, Jeroboam became a threat to Solomon, who tried to kill him. But Jeroboam fled to Egypt, under the protection of the pharaoh, Shishak, and remained there until Solomon's death.

Q Why did Ahijah tear his robe into 12 pieces? 1 Kings 11

A When Jeroboam was still the trusted servant of Solomon, with no thought of disloyalty in his head, he met the Prophet Ahijah in the country outside Jerusalem. Ahijah told him what the future held—that he would become king of Israel, leaving only Judah to Solomon's descendants. As a symbol of what was to happen, Ahijah tore his robe—it was a new one, the Bible tells us—into 12 pieces, representing the Twelve Tribes of Israel. He gave ten pieces to Jeroboam—the ten tribes he would rule over. The two remaining pieces represented Judah and Benjamin, most of the tribe of Benjamin remaining loyal to the House of David.

Throughout the Old Testament, there is a constant struggle to maintain loyalty to the one God. Nearly all the neighbors of the Israelites worshiped a variety of gods, usually in the form of idols.

What were clothes made of in ancient Israel?

In Old Testament times, the clothes of ordinary people were usually made of wool, plenty of which was produced in Palestine. Richer people might wear linen, which was probably imported from Egypt or Edom, although a little flax (from which linen is made) was grown locally. The Bible refers several times to especially fine clothes—such as those which Pharaoh gave to Joseph—being made of linen.

Cotton, which in later times became the most common material for clothes in the region, was unknown in Palestine in the time of King Solomon, and was not even grown in Egypt until one or two centuries later. Silk, though quite common in China, was also non-existent in Solomon's Israel, though it is mentioned in the time of Ezekiel (6th century BC).

What was a shekel?

Money in the form of metal coins did not exist in Palestine in the time of Solomon, and the Israelites probably knew nothing about money in this form until the Babylonian exile. The usual method of payment was barter—exchanging goods of one sort for goods of another sort—and this continued for centuries, even after coins came into use.

Mention of money in the Old Testament can be confusing because the names given to certain values in money were originally weights. When David paid 600 shekels for the threshing floor in Jerusalem where the Temple was to be built, he actually paid gold which weighed 600 shekels.

The Babylonian weight known as a shekel was equal to about $\frac{1}{2}$ ounce (14 g). The silver Hebrew coin that came into use in the 2nd century BC weighed one shekel.

How did farmers store water?

Until the present century, Palestine was always badly affected by lack of water—low rainfall, few rivers, frequent droughts. Modern irrigation methods have worked wonders, but it was a very difficult land even to irrigate by older methods. A good water supply was a precious commodity, and was often the reason for the existence of a particular town or city. The well was the center of every village, and wells are often mentioned in the Bible because they played such an important part in people's lives.

Farmers, as well as city folk, stored water in underground cisterns, carved out of the natural rock. These usually consisted of a narrow shaft descending to a larger chamber. The walls were plastered, and the top was covered with a stone.

When did Israel and Judah become divided? 1 Kings 12

Solomon may have been very wise, and he was certainly very grand. However, he cannot really be called a successful ruler because, after his death in (probably) 922 BC, most of the kingdom supported Jeroboam, the young man who had been promised 10 of the 12 tribes to rule over. Solomon had forced men to work hard and long on his great building projects, and he had also levied heavy taxes. His son and successor, Rehoboam, instead of agreeing to lighten the burdens on the people, warned them that he intended to be a harsher ruler than his father, which ended any hope he had of regaining the whole kingdom.

Thus the kingdom was split in two, with Jeroboam reigning over Israel in the north and Rehoboam reigning over the much smaller country of Judah in the south. This division was never healed.

Who was Zimri? 1 Kings 16

Although Jeroboam first appeared as a hero, later remarks about him in the Bible are critical, and altogether the kings of Israel were not a very admirable line.

In the reign of Elah, a *coup d'état* was attempted by an army commander, Zimri, whose command included half the kingdom's chariots. The king was a drunkard, and one day, when he was drinking heavily in the house of his steward, Zimri broke in and killed him.

He became king himself, and swiftly murdered all Elah's relatives. Unfortunately for him, there were other rivals.

At this time, the army was in the field, fighting the Philistines, and when they heard of the death of Elah, the soldiers voted to make their commander, Omri, king. Omri and his men besieged Tirzah (then capital of the northern kingdom of Israel) and captured it. Zimri withdrew to the royal palace, set it on fire, and died in the flames. His reign had lasted all of seven days.

Who was fed by ravens? 1 Kings 17

Elijah first appears when he is sent by God to King Ahab with a warning of a coming drought.

After he had delivered his warning, he was guided by God to take shelter in a well-hidden cave, near a certain stream. (Although people lived in houses, caves were still sometimes used as temporary homes.) There he was fed morning and evening by ravens, and he drank from the stream until it dried up in the drought.

According to the Bible, the drought is supposed to have lasted three years. Other sources record a drought in Palestine lasting one year.

At last, Elijah went to see Ahab. He reminded him that Jezebel, Ahab's wife, had been worshiping Baal, and killing the Prophets of the true God. Then he told him to gather all the Prophets of Baal together, so that they could prove who was the true God.

God told Elijah, "I have commanded the ravens to feed thee."

Q Who were the Prophets? 1 Kings 17

A In the modern meaning, a prophet is someone who foretells the future, but the Prophets of ancient Israel were not simply fortune tellers. Originally, they did little prophesying. A Prophet such as Samuel was a national holy man, a kind of priest, the keeper of the nation's conscience and the mouthpiece of God. This was also true of Elijah and his successors. What Elijah did was to express what he felt was the will of God in a particular situation, which is not the same as forecasting the weather or movements in the stock market.

Prophets could be of humble birth. Elisha, successor to Elijah, was the son of a farmer; Amos was a shepherd. They felt themselves to be the spiritual leaders of the nation, with a special commission from God, and as a rule they lived among the people, not removing themselves from the world like monks.

A "prophet" was not an official position, like a priest. The major Prophets were men of powerful personality.

Q How did Elijah defeat the prophets of Baal? 1 Kings 18

A After gathering the people at Mount Carmel, Elijah issued a challenge to the priests of Baal. Each side should build an altar and prepare a sacrifice for a burnt offering. The fire should not be lit, but the priests of Baal—there were 450 of them—should call on their god to light the fire, and Elijah would call on his.

Baal failed to deliver a spark, prompting sarcastic comments from Elijah. When it was Elijah's turn, Yahweh sent fire from heaven that burned up the bull that Elijah had chosen as a sacrifice, as well as the wood and the stones and earth round about.

The Israelites proclaimed their belief in Yahweh, and Elijah ordered the slaughter of the priests of Baal.

This is a typically heroic story, showing Elijah, the greatest of the Prophets before Isaiah, in action. It is typical, too, in showing him engaged in the constant task of the Prophets—to keep Israel on the right religious road. However, it does give a misleading

who is the chief villain in the stories about Ahab and Elijah. The priests of Baal, with whom Elijah had his great contest, were Jezebel's priests, and after they had been killed on Elijah's orders, Jezebel sent a message to Elijah promising that he would be dead in the same way within 24 hours.

Jezebel also arranged the death of Naboth, and this story suggests another way in which she was a divisive element. She was used to another form of kingship, more common in the Middle East, in which the king was always right and was regarded as almost a god himself. This was far from the tradition in Israel, where God's covenant was made with the people and kings were comparative newcomers.

 How did God's voice come to Elijah? 1 Kings 19

 After receiving Jezebel's threat against his life, Elijah went by himself into the desert, eventually as far as Sinai, the place where Moses had received the Ten Commandments. There he sheltered in a cave. The word of the Lord came to him, telling him to go outside and stand upon the mountain, for the Lord was passing by. There was a great wind that shattered the rocks, but God was not in the wind. There was an earthquake, but God was not in the earthquake, a fire, but he was not in the fire.

Then there came a low murmuring sound, a still, small voice of calm. And it was the voice of God.

impression of the relations between Baal and Yahweh, which were closer than this story suggests. In fact, many people did not distinguish between Baal and Yahweh, regarding them as one and the same.

 What was as small as "a man's hand"? 1 Kings 18

 Whose wife was Jezebel?

 Born in Tyre, of Phoenician descent, Jezebel was the wife of Ahab, king of Israel from about 869 to 850 BC. She is an evil figure in the Bible, and it is Jezebel, rather than her husband Ahab,

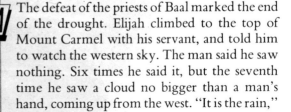 The defeat of the priests of Baal marked the end of the drought. Elijah climbed to the top of Mount Carmel with his servant, and told him to watch the western sky. The man said he saw nothing. Six times he said it, but the seventh time he saw a cloud no bigger than a man's hand, coming up from the west. "It is the rain," said Elijah.

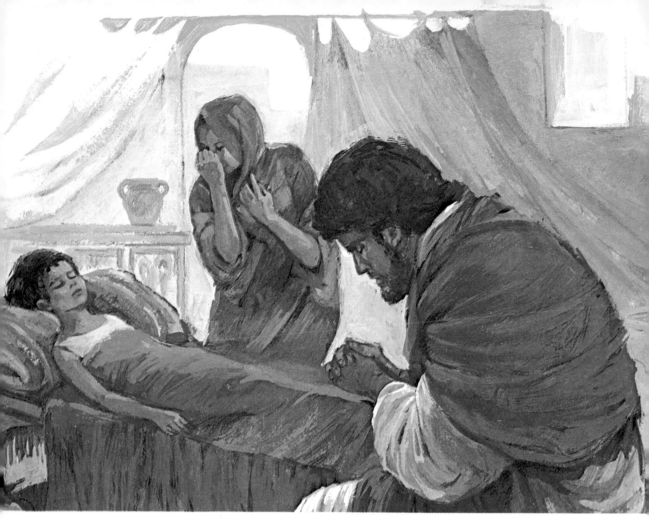

Elijah prays over the widow's son.

to God for his life to be restored. The child breathed again, and Elijah returned him to his mother.

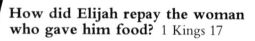

How did Elijah repay the woman who gave him food? 1 Kings 17

During the drought, when Elijah had to leave his cave because the stream had dried up, God told him to go to a certain village. There he saw a widow gathering firewood, and he asked her for water and bread. She brought him water, but said she had only a handful of flour left in the jar and a little oil in the flask. She was gathering wood to cook a last meal for her son and herself, before they died of starvation. Elijah asked her to make him a small cake anyway, and after that to make something for herself and her son. For, he said, the jar of flour and the flask of oil would not run out until after the drought had ended.

Later, the widow's son died, but Elijah took the child up to the roof of the house and prayed

What kind of food was eaten in Old Testament times?

The food of ordinary people was simple, but it was reasonably varied and quite nourishing. The cheapest, most basic food was bread made from barley, baked in flat loaves in a clay oven. Sometimes cakes were baked from barley meal and sweetened with honey or figs (refined sugar was unknown). Butter and cheese were made from goats' milk, but meat was a luxury for most people. Meat came from sheep, goats and oxen; pork and camel meat were forbidden. Chickens were eaten, as well as eggs. Fish from the Jordan River were usually salted and dried so they could be stored. A great many vegetables were available, such as beans, peas, lentils, onions, leeks, lettuce, beets, cucumbers, garlic and other herbs and spices, and there was plenty of fruit in season, mainly figs, dates, melons and pomegranates. Grapes were widely grown for wine, and olives for their oil.

Why was Naboth killed? 1 Kings 21

Naboth was the owner of a vineyard near King Ahab's royal palace. Ahab wanted the vineyard to turn it into a vegetable garden, and offered to buy it. Naboth refused, saying he could not sell the inheritance of his forefathers. Ahab left, cross and grumpy.

Jezebel, his wife, came to the king and tried to cheer him up, saying she would get Naboth's vineyard for him since Ahab could not. She wrote a letter in Ahab's name, instructing the Elders of the town where Naboth lived to hire a few scoundrels who would accuse him of blaspheming against God and the king. This would give them an excuse to have Naboth stoned to death.

All this was done, and Ahab gained possession of Naboth's vineyard.

What did Elijah prophesy in the vineyard?

While Ahab was still admiring his new possession, God sent Elijah to Naboth's vineyard to warn Ahab that because of his wickedness in taking the property after killing the owner, disaster would fall upon him and his descendants: "Where the dogs licked the blood of Naboth, there shall they lick your blood also." And so it happened.

Why was Ahab annoyed by Micaiah? 1 Kings 22

Ahab joined with Jehosaphat to attack Syria in order to regain the border province of Ramoth-Gilead. Before the attack began, Ahab consulted 400 prophets. With one voice, they advised him to carry out the attack, saying God would give him the city. Jehosaphat, perhaps thinking that this was a case of people giving the advice that the king wanted to hear, was cautious, and asked if there was anyone else they should consult. There was only one other prophet, Ahab said, and that was Micaiah, a gloomy fellow who was always forecasting doom. However, he sent someone to get him.

Micaiah, knowing what all the others had said, told Ahab to attack. But he did not sound sincere, and Ahab demanded that he speak the truth. Micaiah then said that he had seen a vision of the Israelites scattered like sheep without a shepherd. Also, he had seen God asking the angels how Ahab could be persuaded to attack Ramoth-Gilead. The answer had been to give him a false prophecy through his prophets.

Ahab ordered Micaiah to be locked up until he returned victorious.

Ahab unwisely goes to war against the Syrians.

How did Ahab die? 1 Kings 22

 Ahab and Jehosaphat went to war against Syria to regain Ramoth-Gilead. Ahab was dressed as an ordinary soldier, so the enemy would not recognize him and concentrate their fire on him. But, by chance, a Syrian arrow struck Ahab at the point where there was a chink in his armor, between shoulder-plate and breastplate. Badly wounded, Ahab told his chariot driver to take him out of the battle line, but he died the same evening. His body was taken home for burial, and his chariot, full of the dead king's blood, was washed out near the place where Naboth had been stoned to death. The dogs came to lick it up, fulfilling the prophesy of Elijah in the vineyard.

It seems strange that Elijah is not mentioned in this story, and the reason is probably that it comes from a different source than the previous chapters, in which Elijah is seen as the greatest Prophet in Israel.

 Why did Elisha refuse to leave Elijah? 2 Kings 2

When Elijah reached the end of his life, he told his friend and disciple, Elisha, who was traveling with him, to leave him. "Stay here," he said, "for the Lord is sending me to Bethel." But Elisha refused. At Bethel, they met a group of prophets, or holy men, who lived there. They said to Elisha, "God is going to take your master away." Elisha replied grimly, "I know." Twice more Elijah tried to shake off the faithful Elisha, but without success, and in the end Elisha was with him when God took him.

Although the Bible does not give any explanation of why Elijah wanted Elisha to go, it seems that Elijah wanted to be alone at the last, though perhaps in the end he was glad of Elisha's company.

 What was Elijah's last gift to Elisha?

 Elijah, accompanied by his disciple Elisha, crossed the River Jordan after the waters parted in the same way that the Red Sea had parted to allow the Israelites to escape from Egypt. On their way across, Elijah asked Elisha to tell him anything he could do for him before he was taken away by God. Elisha asked that he should inherit a double measure of Elijah's spirit. A hard request, Elijah said, "but if you see me taken from you, it shall be granted."

Then came a whirlwind, and Elijah was carried up to heaven amid chariots of fire. And the spirit of Elijah settled on Elisha.

Because Elijah had been taken up into heaven, and had never "died," it came to be believed that he would one day reappear. In the New Testament, some people believed that John the Baptist was Elijah, come again.

 Did the Israelites believe in life after death?

 For most of the period covered in the Old Testament, there is no real sign of a belief in an afterlife in the Hebrew religion. The life of the individual person did not seem so important to the Israelites as it does to us. They thought more of the survival of groups—the family and the nation. It was vital to them to have sons to carry on the family line.

Ideas began to change during the Exile in Babylon. Because families and the nation were broken up, the existence of the individual person came to seem more important. By the time of the Book of Daniel, there is a clear belief in life after death.

This grew stronger during the time of the Maccabees in the 2nd and 1st centuries BC. There were many Jewish heroes and martyrs, and it seemed that, if God was a just god, these people would surely be rewarded by life after death.

 What kind of pottery was made in ancient Israel?

Pottery was made in Palestine thousands of years before the Israelites settled there, but the Israelites themselves made no pottery until they settled down and gave up their nomadic life.

Pottery was an important craft, and there are many references to it in the Bible. A great variety of bowls, jars and jugs were made,

Pottery was an important craft in early human societies. Vessels were made of clay long before metals came into use.

including very large vessels in which olive oil or wine was stored. Grain, too, was stored in earthenware containers.

Although all pottery was simply intended to be useful, it was often decorated with designs made while the clay was still soft. Egyptian potters, among others, had learned how to glaze their pottery—baking on a hard, glassy surface—but this was not done in Palestine. There the potters gave a smooth, shiny finish to the vessel by rubbing it with shell or a stone while it turned on the potter's wheel.

 Who were the Syrians?

Syria was the country to the north and east of Palestine. In the Bible it is often called Aram, and the people Aramaeans. Its main city was Damascus, which is still the capital of the modern republic of Syria. The size of the country varied a good deal at different times, but it was larger and richer than Palestine. It was ruled by a succession of conquerors, and life in Syria was more sophisticated than life in Palestine.

Syrian influences on Palestine—and, therefore, the Israelites—were very strong. The Syrians, or Aramaeans, were often enemies of the Israelites, especially of the northern kingdom of Israel, although they were regarded as being distantly related. It was among the Aramaeans that Abraham looked for a wife for his son Isaac. The Aramaic language had become the common tongue in Palestine by the time of Jesus, as it was throughout most of the Middle East.

 What disease did Naaman suffer from? 2 Kings 5

Naaman was the Syrian general who suffered from the disease of leprosy. His wife's maid was an Israelite girl, and she advised him to consult the Prophet Elisha. He told Naaman to wash in the River Jordan. Naaman was not impressed —the Jordan seemed to him a small and muddy river—but his servants persuaded him to do as Elisha said, and he was cured.

Leprosy is a chronic and infectious disease, which affects the skin and the nerves. It was incurable, though some people did recover from it. Lepers were forced to live outside the town. Probably Naaman's case was not yet serious, as it did not affect his normal life nor prevent him holding high command under the Syrian king. It was, perhaps, not the disease we today call leprosy—the word was applied to many similar complaints—and people must have believed it to be non-infectious.

How did Gehazi discover the price of greed? 2 Kings 5

Naaman was so pleased when he saw that he had been cured of leprosy because he followed Elisha's advice that he offered the Prophet gold and silver. Elisha had no interest in wealth and refused it. But his servant, Gehazi, overheard, and he thought it an awful waste not to accept such treasure.

After Naaman had left, Gehazi slipped away and rode after him. When he caught up with Naaman, Gehazi said that, just after the general had left, two young disciples had come to visit Elisha, and although the Prophet wanted nothing himself, he would be grateful if Naaman could spare a little money for them. Naaman gave him more than he asked, not suspecting the trick.

But Elisha knew what Gehazi had done, and told him that, in getting gold and silver from Naaman, he had got leprosy, too. All at once Gehazi found that he was suffering from the symptoms of the disease.

Who threw Jezebel from a window? 2 Kings 9

The doom pronounced on Ahab by Elijah extended to all his family. That doom was brought about by the general, Jehu, who, on the directions of Elijah, was anointed as king of Israel. He was told that he must destroy Ahab's family, because Ahab had persecuted the Prophets and worshipped Baal. Jehu had been fighting in the campaign against Syria in which the two kingdoms of Israel and Judah were fighting as allies.

Jehu rapidly killed the kings of Israel and Judah, who were Ahab's son and nephew. Then he rode furiously to Jezreel where Jezebel, Ahab's widow, was still living. She defied him from a high window in the palace. Jehu called up to the window, "Who is on my side?" A few courtiers, standing near Jezebel, signaled their support, and Jehu shouted, "Throw her down!" They pitched the evil queen out of the window. Her body was trampled by horses and eaten by dogs, so that when they came to bury it, there was hardly anything left.

This savage story is witness to the Israelites' hatred of heresy—for the crime of Jezebel and the two murdered kings was, above all, that they were worshipers of Baal.

Why were wells so important?

Water is the great necessity of life. No one can live for long without it. But Palestine is a very dry country, some of it being so dry that it is desert. The well—the water supply for all the inhabitants—was the center of the village, rather like the village inn in later times. When a new well was dug, it was an occasion for feasting and dancing.

Wells could also be the cause of quarrels, especially in the early days, when the Israelites were still mainly nomadic. In Genesis, we hear of conflict over the famous wells of Beersheba in Abraham's time, and again in Isaac's. Isaac's servant met Rebekah at a well, which was a meeting place for those who would not otherwise have any contact with each other.

Q What kinds of musical instruments were played in Old Testament times?

A Music probably played a big part in the life of the Israelites. The Book of Psalms is, in fact, a book of hymns which were sung as part of services of worship. Some of the Psalms are believed to have been written by David (see page 68), who was an accomplished musician.

The instrument he played was a simple harp or lyre, a stringed instrument which was plucked. We cannot be certain what this or other instruments looked like, although some examples have been unearthed by archeologists.

Among other instruments mentioned in the Bible are: pipes, made of reed or bronze; a larger form of lyre (David's "harp" could be played while walking); trumpets; and cymbals, rattles and other percussion instruments, including drums.

Q Who were the Assyrians?

A The Assyrians were a vigorous and warlike people originating in northern Mesopotamia, who created an empire extending, at its greatest, across much of the Middle East, from Egypt to Persia. The Israelites were afraid of them—and with good reason, because Assyrian kings often raided Israel and Judah. The Assyrians took advantage of the division between the two kingdoms, and eventually destroyed the northern kingdom. They seriously damaged the southern kingdom (Judah), but they never succeeded in capturing its capital, Jerusalem.

Musical instruments: (a) a cymbal consisting of two brass bowls which could be struck against each other; (b) a portable drum; (c) a sistrum, a kind of metal rattle; (d) flutes.

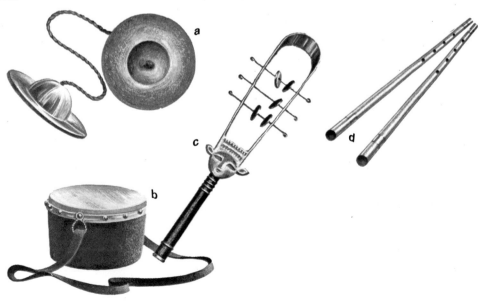

Q What prevented Sennacherib from capturing Jerusalem? 2 Kings 19

A In the eyes of God, Hezekiah was the best king since David, because he reformed religion, destroying the idols of Baal and other survivals of the Canaanite religion. He was the king of Judah around 700 BC, and information is given about him in the Book of Chronicles and in Isaiah, as well as the Second Book of Kings. The first part of his reign was very successful, a time of prosperity in which he gained control of the Philistine territory on the coastal plain of Palestine. Later, he came under severe pressure from the Assyrians.

Hezekiah rebelled against the Assyrians, and King Sennacherib marched into Judah, taking city after city. As he advanced on Jerusalem, Hezekiah tried to buy him off, sending lavish tribute of gold and silver—even stripping the gold from the doors of the Temple. However, the Assyrians continued to advance.

God had promised that Jerusalem would not fall, and at night, "the angel of the Lord went out and struck down 185,000 men in the Assyrian camp." As a result, Sennacherib was forced to withdraw. He returned to Nineveh,

his capital, where not long afterward he was murdered.

In ancient times (and much later), the greatest menace to an army in the field was often not the enemy, but disease. Clearly some epidemic struck Sennacherib's army, possibly bubonic plague.

 ## Who was Isaiah?

The Book of Isaiah is the longest prophetic book in the Old Testament, but it was not all written by the same man. The first Isaiah, one of the greatest of the Hebrew Prophets, was born about 765 BC and lived in Jerusalem. He

The task of the Prophet in Israelite society was to keep the people loyal to the Covenant.

was called to be a Prophet in a dramatic vision, which is described in Chapter 6. Isaiah lived close to the center of power. He knew every inch of the Temple, and he was the counselor of kings—especially of Ahaz and Hezekiah.

Isaiah was such a great man that two later works, which were written by Prophets whose names we do not know, were added to his Book. The "second Isaiah" (Chapters 40–55) lived nearly 200 years later. The "third Isaiah" (Chapters 56–66) another 100 years after that.

What was the sign that Hezekiah would not die? 2 Kings 20

After he had reigned for 14 years, Hezekiah became sick, and Isaiah told him he was going to die. But the King prayed to God, and before Isaiah had left the palace, God told him that Hezekiah would be given another 15 years of life. As a sign that this was true, God caused the shadow of the pillar which acted as the palace sundial, casting a shadow on a flight of steps, to go backward for ten steps.

  What sacrifices were made to Moloch?

Moloch, or Molech, was a god worshiped by the Ammonites and others. The worship of Moloch is said to have been introduced to Israel by several Israelite kings, and according to the author of the Second Book of Kings, it was the reason for the downfall of the northern kingdom.

The best-known aspect of Moloch worship was the sacrifice of children as burnt offerings. This practice was forbidden by Hebrew law and was punishable by death. However, at times the Israelites seem to have felt compelled to sacrifice their first-born children (Abraham's near-sacrifice of Isaac is the most famous example). Several Prophets, including Jeremiah, furiously attacked this frightful practice, and according to the law of Moses, anyone performing this sacrifice was executed.

  Who was Nebuchadnezzar?

Nebuchadnezzar II, the Great, was king of New Babylon from 605 to 562 BC. (It is called "New Babylon" because there was an earlier Babylonian empire, "Old Babylon," which was a great power before the Assyrians; New Babylon succeeded the Assyrian empire.) He was one of the most able rulers of his line, and is a great figure in ancient history. So far as the Israelites were concerned, Nebuchadnezzar is remembered as the king who occupied Judah and, after King Jehoiakim had rebelled, destroyed the kingdom and carried off most of its people to exile in Babylon.

Above, the Temple at Jerusalem, destroyed by Nebuchadnezzar in 586 BC.

Below, Nebuchadnezzar threatens to kill his wise men, when they cannot interpret his dream, (see page 98).

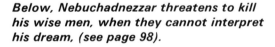

How was Israel destroyed? 2 Kings 18

Of the two kingdoms, Israel, the northern kingdom, was destroyed first. Judah survived over a century longer.

At the time when the good king Hezekiah ruled over Judah and rooted out the worship of false gods, the northern kingdom was in a terrible state. Although Yahweh was still worshiped, he was worshiped in the form of idols, which was forbidden by the Second Commandment. The Israelites, who were cut off from the heart of their religion in the Temple in Jerusalem, also prayed to many other gods. It was for this reason, the Bible says, that God decided to destroy Israel.

His instrument was Shalmanezer V, king of Assyria in about 725 BC. He made the northern kingdom a tribute state, but his demands were so harsh that the Israelites, in alliance with Egypt (the only other great power in the region), rebelled. This provoked a full-scale Assyrian attack. Samaria, then the capital, fell after a long siege, and many were carried off to other parts of the Assyrian empire. They were replaced by people of other races, who became the people known later as the Samaritans.

Who ruled the Assyrians?

The warlike kings of Assyria had impressive-sounding names such as Tiglath-Pileser, Shalmanezer, Sennacherib, Assurbanipal. The successor of Shalmanezer V was Sargon II, who reigned from 722 to 705 BC. He completed the task of taking Israel captive, forcing thousands of people into exile in other parts of the Assyrian empire.

Babylon was a magnificent city, with great walls and gates, (like this reconstruction of the Gate of Ishtar).

worship of false gods, and the kings that came after him failed to follow his example—until, that is, the reign of Josiah, which began in about 640 BC.

Josiah carried out reforms even more drastic than those of Hezekiah. He was impelled and guided in this program by the discovery in the Temple, while it was being repaired, of an old Book of the Law. This seems to have been the Book we know as Deuteronomy, perhaps the most important collection of Moses's Law, most of which had been written down in the reign of Manasseh, son of Hezekiah (some parts, however, were added later). Thanks to this discovery, such things as the Feast of the Passover were restored to their proper place in religious worship.

Shaphan was the official who found the book, or at least took it to Hezekiah. He was probably also involved in the work of reform which followed.

Q What was the Babylonian Captivity?

A When Syria and the northern kingdom of Israel fell to the Assyrians, it seemed only a matter of time before Judah also fell. However, in the late 7th century BC, the Assyrian empire itself collapsed, rather unexpectedly, under attack from the people who founded the empire known as New Babylon. (The history of the Babylonians and Assyrians is often intertwined, over many centuries.)

The Babylonians were just as formidable as the Assyrians, and in due course, Judah fell to them. As was the usual practice of conquerors in ancient times, the inhabitants of the conquered kingdom—or a great many of them—were carried off—in this case, to Babylon. This policy was designed to make rebellions less likely. The period during which the people (who were now formally known as the Jews) were held in Babylon is called the Babylonian Captivity.

Q What is the Book of Deuteronomy?

A The Book of Deuteronomy (which means "the Second Law") is the last of the five books which make up the Pentateuch, or the Law (Torah) in the Old Testament. Tradition ascribes it to Moses, but the laws it gives, which cover a wide range of both religious and civil matters, seem to belong to a settled community, not the semi-nomadic people of which Moses was the leader. It was, in fact, probably written by priests of Jerusalem under the influence of the great Prophets, eager to raise the moral standard of life in Israel. It is likely that the core of the Book of Deuteronomy is the Book of the Law discovered in the Temple by Shaphan, which was written about 50 years earlier, in the reign of King Manasseh. It was the basis for the sweeping reforms of King Josiah.

Q What did Shaphan find in the Temple? 2 Kings 22

A The disasters that befell the Israelites were interpreted as the punishment of God. Even Hezekiah had not succeeded in rooting out all

Q How did Josiah try to save Judah?

A Reading the Book of the Law which Shaphan had brought him, King Josiah was horrified to see how God's commands had been ignored and his laws broken, and equally horrified to read of the dreadful things that would happen

Under Josiah's rule, false gods and idols were destroyed.

to the people if they did ignore God's commands. One of the disasters forecast was that their children would disappear into captivity.

Josiah made every effort to restore God's word, obey his laws and ensure that all of the people did so, too. He got rid of all heathen priests and images, burned idols, and destroyed the shrines and temples of Baal and other false gods.

God relented only to the extent that he postponed the punishment of Judah until after Josiah's death, because Josiah had repented when he read the Book of the Law.

Thirteen years after Shaphan's discovery, Josiah was killed in battle. His successors fell back into the old ways, and Judah was in due course punished by the Babylonian Captivity.

Q Who was Ashtoreth?

A When Josiah was carrying out his religious reforms—the worship of Baal was going on in the precincts of the Temple itself, we learn—he destroyed hill shrines in the east of Jerusalem, on the Mount of Olives, which were dedicated to Ashtoreth. The Bible says that they had been erected by Solomon and describes Ashtoreth as a "loathsome" goddess of the people of Sidon.

Ashtoreth (the name is also spelled "Asherah" and in other ways; it means "Lady of the Sea") is mentioned many times in the Old Testament. She was a Phoenician goddess, and her shrines were probably patronized by Solomon for diplomatic reasons.

We are told (1 Samuel 31) that after Saul was killed his armour was placed in a temple of Ashtoreth. But she is found in various forms among many peoples of the ancient Middle East, and often appears as an equivalent of the Greek goddess Aphrodite (Venus, to the Romans).

What happened in the valley of Hinnom?

The valley of Hinnom ran south and west of Jerusalem and formed the boundary between the tribes of Benjamin and Judah. It seems that there was a sanctuary here to Moloch, where children were burned as a sacrifice to the god. In the account of the destruction of shrines to false gods by the reforming king Josiah, this is one of the places mentioned (2 Kings 23).

What kind of fruit was eaten in Palestine?

In ancient Israel, fruit was sometimes eaten at the end of a meal. The most common types were figs, dates, melons, and pomegranates. Figs were especially prized for their sweetness because sugar was unknown. Every household had a fig tree and probably a vine. Pomegranates were the equivalent of apples, and they are often mentioned in the Bible. They were squeezed for their juice, and sometimes wine was made from them. Grapes were the usual basis for wine, but they do not seem to have often been eaten as fruit, though they were eaten dried as raisins.

Who was Job?

The Book of Job, which was probably written about 400 BC, tells a story of a kind that is also to be found in the mythology of other societies. It is the story of the good man who suffers a long series of hardships but is rewarded in the end. The story confirms the well-known saying, "Patience is a virtue."

But although the story of Job is basically an ancient folk story, the Book of Job in the Bible is much more than that. In the first place, it is a poem and, in the opinion of many experts, the finest long poem in the Hebrew Bible. It also contains interesting theological questions. For example, the author, who remains quite unknown in spite of much scholarly research, clearly does not believe in the long-accepted idea that suffering is the result of sin—since Job is not sinful. Job comes to accept God's will, without question and without complaint, and

after that his health, money and family are restored to him.

What is the Book of Proverbs?

The Book of Proverbs is a collection of wise sayings. According to tradition, they are the sayings of Solomon, who was renowned for his wisdom. Some of them may well date back to the time of Solomon, but the Book of Proverbs was compiled much later. On the whole, it is not very polite about kings, which seems to rule out Solomon's authorship.

Proverbs is a sort of textbook, which instructs people how to live in the right way, and teaches that wisdom lies in reverence for God and obedience to God's laws. However, it is not only religious; it contains much practical wisdom, too.

Who was the first Prophet to write a book?

Probably none of the Prophets ever sat down to write his prophecies himself. This task was undertaken by a disciple or scribe, who recorded the Prophet's sayings. Amos, who lived in the 8th century BC, was the first to have his sayings collected in a single book, and apart from a few verses which were probably put in at a later date, it is clearly the work of one man —the personality of Amos comes out strongly.

Nothing is known of Amos except what we can learn from his book. The reason his prophecies were written down was possibly that his message could not be passed on in any other way. He lived at a time of prosperity, yet his message was a grim one, forecasting doom and gloom and carrying the threat that God might forsake his own Chosen People.

What kind of men became prophets?

The Hebrew word for "prophet" means a "preacher inspired by God." The prophets believed that God had revealed his secrets to them and they must teach these to the people.

Prophets did not belong to any particular class, like priests; in fact, they could be men of humble birth. Amos is said to have been a simple herdsman.

The word "prophet" makes us think of great figures like Isaiah or Elijah, who seem to have been the greatest men in Israel in their day. But prophets were more numerous than this. We hear of bands of them—Ahab summoned 400 when he wanted advice on going to war—and they sometimes lived in communities of their own (like the prophets at Bethel at the end of Elijah's life). But they remained in contact with the people. They did not keep separate, like some types of monks.

For much of the historical period covered by the Old Testament, it was the Prophets who gave Israel its great spiritual strength. Without them, especially from the 8th century BC onwards, there would have been rather little to admire in Israel.

What were seals used for?

A seal is both an object for making an impression on a clay tablet, and the impression itself. It served the same purpose as a signature on a document.

There were two kinds of seal in use, stamp seals and cylinder seals. Cylinder seals, the usual type in Mesopotamia, were rolled over the clay, and a relatively large "picture" would appear. In Palestine, stamp seals, with simple raised, flat surfaces (like those found on signet rings), were more common.

For us today, seals are important because they form the most interesting and informative group of objects from ancient civilizations in the Middle East which archeologists have found. Many thousands of them have survived, some dating from over 5,000 years ago. A number of them are marvelous little works of art, but all are of interest for the signs, pictures, figures and other designs they bear.

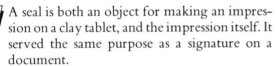

Were the Prophets always men?

All the most famous prophets were men, but women could be prophets, or prophetesses, too. When King Josiah, after hearing what was written in the Book of Law, wanted to know if there was anything that could be done to

prevent the fate which the Book said would fall upon those who ignored God's commands, he sent for a prophetess named Huldah. Several other female prophets are mentioned in the Old Testament, including Miriam (Moses's sister), Deborah in the Book of Judges (Chapter 4), and Noadiah. Prophets could have wives, and their wives were sometimes known as prophetesses.

In New Testament times, female prophets seem to have been more numerous. They probably formed groups or communities, as male prophets did in earlier years.

When did Judah become Judea?
Ezra 9

The country once known as Judah, originally the land of the tribe of Judah, started to be called Judea by about 500 BC. This name simply means "land of the Jews," the name that the people formerly known as Hebrews or Israelites had by that time acquired. Judea was then a province of the Persian empire, and the name referred to the district centered on Jerusalem, whose boundaries often altered.

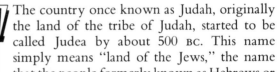

Who was the saddest of the Prophets?

It was the job of the Prophets to keep people loyal to the worship of God and to warn what would happen if they did not. As a result, the major Prophets seem to have spent a great deal of their time uttering terrible warnings of the dreadful things that were about to happen to the Israelites as a result of their sinfulness. No Prophet had a grimmer message than Jeremiah.

However, that was not his fault. Although Jeremiah was one of the greatest and most appealing of the major Prophets, the circumstances of his time seemed to offer little hope. He was active after the death of Josiah, when everything was going wrong—the destruction of Jerusalem (including the Temple), the ruin of Judah and the captivity of its people. Because he preached submission to the king of Babylon (undoubtedly the wisest policy), he was regarded as a traitor.

Q What kind of place was Babylon?

A Babylon, the capital of the Babylonian empire, was a great city. Although the original city was destroyed by the Assyrians in 689 BC, it was rebuilt, and under King Nebuchadnezzar it had a reputation for great splendor. It stood on both banks of the River Euphrates, in what is now southern Iraq, and several bridges linked the two sides of the city. It was surrounded by great walls, and contained massive temples and

An impression of the Hanging Gardens of Babylon

palaces. The area enclosed by the outer wall is said to have been about 200 sq miles (320 sq kilometers), although this was probably an exaggeration. The great buildings were made of brick and richly colored.

The walls were so broad that they acted as a road: chariots could be driven along the top. Otherwise, people could move around the city by canal.

Who built the Hanging Gardens?

The Hanging Gardens of Babylon were one of the Seven Wonders of the ancient world. They were built about 600 BC by King Nebuchadnezzar for his wife, Amytis, who was homesick for the mountains of her native land, in what is now Iran. The gardens must have consisted of a series of terraces, rising to a height of about 330 ft (100 meters) and planted with exotic trees and flowers. Archeologists think they have found the remains of the Hanging Gardens, although what is left does not seem to be grand enough to explain the great fame of Nebuchadnezzar's creation in ancient times.

Who rescued Jeremiah from the pit? Jeremiah 38

For his courage in speaking the word of God and for warning the people of the fate in store for them, Jeremiah was poorly rewarded. He was imprisoned, tortured, and nearly killed more than once. His warning that Jerusalem would be captured by the king of Babylon particularly annoyed the army commanders, who feared such talk would destroy morale among the soldiers. They therefore lowered him into a pit of mud, which was in the courtyard of the guard house and was possibly a disused water cistern. Jeremiah would not have lived long down there but for an Ethiopian, who told the king about it. King Zedekiah then gave orders that Jeremiah should be pulled out.

Who wrote down Jeremiah's prophecies?

While Jeremiah was in prison because he rebuked the king, he summoned his friend and disciple, Baruch, to bring ink and rolls of papyrus and to write down what he said. Baruch seems to have been a man of some social standing, though we know little about him. He is mentioned several times in the Book of Jeremiah, although the Book as it exists in the Bible today probably contains some material that was not written down by him.

In the Apocrypha, (see page 108) there is a Book of Baruch, which was written in Hebrew at a somewhat later time—no one knows exactly when. It is possible that some parts of it are based on sayings of Jeremiah's friend.

What did Jeremiah learn from the potter? Jeremiah 18

At one time, God told Jeremiah to go down to the potter's house, where he would tell Jeremiah what he had to say. Jeremiah obeyed, and found the potter working at his wheel. The Prophet watched the craftsman smoothing and shaping the clay as it revolved on the wheel. He saw that sometimes it did not come out right, and when that happened, the potter would discard it and start again.

Then God spoke to Jeremiah. Just as the potter could destroy and remold his clay vessel, so God could destroy and remold a nation.

What kind of art did the Israelites have?

The making of images was forbidden by the Ten Commandments and, as a result, there was no painting or sculpture as we know it in ancient Israel. What did exist was imported from other societies, and figures like the cherubim in the Temple were probably the work of Phoenician artists. So were statues of Baal and other heathen gods which, judging by the criticism of the Prophets, were at times quite numerous.

Nor were the spiritual leaders interested in architecture. Architectural ideas—for instance,

for the building of the Temple in Jerusalem—came from Mesopotamia or Egypt. Too much grandeur was frowned on by religious people.

What are the Lamentations?

The Book of Lamentations is sometimes called the Lamentations of Jeremiah, who is named as the author in the Greek version but not in the original Hebrew version. The style is quite different from the Book of Jeremiah, and it is unlikely that this is the work of the Prophet, although it must have been composed about the same time.

The Book of Lamentations begins with a series of poems lamenting the destruction of Jerusalem, and it seems obvious that the author must have seen this terrible event happen. What was so terrible was not simply the destruction of a capital city, or even the destruction of the Temple, but the fact that God had forsaken his people.

These poems are still read in synagogues today to mark the destruction of the Temple—both Solomon's Temple and the later Temple destroyed by the Romans.

When did Jerusalem fall?

The kingdom of Judah was already in serious decline. Some of its citizens had been deported to Babylon when, in 587 BC Nebuchadnezzar's Babylonian army, after a long siege, broke through Jerusalem's walls. The events leading up to this disaster, caused by a nationalist rebellion, were the cause of Jeremiah's anguished warnings.

According to the account in the Second Book of Kings (Chapter 25), the Temple and all the houses were burned and the walls broken down. The bronze pillars outside the Temple were broken up and the metal taken to Babylon, along with other valuables. The citizens, those who were well-off and those who had any special skill, were deported to Babylon. Only those with no skill or money were left.

The Babylonian army besieged Jerusalem, and after it fell, people were forced into exile in Babylon.

What happened to Ezekiel when Jerusalem fell?

Ezekiel, who grew up in a priestly family in Jerusalem, was one of the earliest exiles to Babylon. He was deported along with King Jehoiachim and the "best" people in Jerusalem in about 597 BC. His early prophecy (he did not become a prophet until he had been in Babylon for five years) was a warning of the coming destruction of Jerusalem and the Temple. There is some evidence in the Book of Ezekiel that the Prophet suffered from some kind of nervous disease, or perhaps epilepsy, and that when the city finally fell and was destroyed by Nebuchadnezzar's troops in 587 BC, Ezekiel was cured of this illness. The terrific strain he had been living under disappeared at last when the deed, terrible though it was, finally happened as he had prophesied.

What was the vision of Ezekiel? Ezekiel 37

The Prophet Ezekiel was among those exiled to Babylon. In his vision, he walked on a plain which was covered with dry bones, bleached by the sun. God asked if those bones could ever live again, and Ezekiel replied that only God could tell that. Then God commanded him to tell the bones to join together, to regain flesh and skin. He did, and the bones turned into bodies, but lifeless ones. Then, following God's instructions, Ezekiel told the wind to breathe life into them, and soon the bodies breathed again, and got up from the ground, and were alive.

Ezekiel's vision was a promise of a better future. At that time, the Jews in exile were like the dead, dry bones, cut off from everything that gave their life meaning. But one day God would restore them to their homes, and breathe new spirit into them.

What happened to the Hebrew religion during the Babylonian Captivity?

We do not know very much about the life of the Jewish exiles in Babylon. Of course they could no longer worship God in the Temple, but they learned to worship him in other ways, meeting together on the Sabbath (at the house of Ezekiel, perhaps) to pray, read the Scriptures and sing hymns. The type of devotions which was developed in exile was the foundation of later worship in the synagogue. In fact, the gatherings for prayer and worship (and not, as at the Temple, for sacrifice) which took place in Babylon were possibly the origin of the idea of the synagogue. However, the word "synagogue" does not appear in the Old Testament.

There is no doubt that the period of exile was very important for the future of Judaism. It was then that many of the Scriptures were written down. Groups such as the Pharisees can also be traced back to this period.

How were fields made on hillsides?

Much of the territory of the Israelites in Palestine was very hilly. It was therefore necessary for farmers to use any suitable land for their crops, and one way in which sloping ground could be used more productively than simply for pasture was by making terraces—a series of wide steps up the hillsides. This type of construction, which prevented the topsoil from washing away, was common in the ancient Middle East, even in buildings. The Tower of Babel and other Mesopotamian temples were in the form of ziggurats, or stepped pyramids. Even the Temple of Jerusalem was built on a platform.

Who wrote the Book of Jonah?

Jonah was a Prophet of the northern kingdom in the reign of Jeroboam II—in the 8th century BC. His book, which is the fifth of the twelve books of the Minor Prophets, is unusual because it relates, not the sayings of the Prophet, but the things that happened to him, such as being swallowed by a whale (which is a story, not history).

In reality, the Book of Jonah was written much later than the time of the Prophet himself, probably between the 6th and the 3rd centuries BC. The author simply made use of Jonah's name. The Book of Jonah is particularly interesting to non-Jews because the author was making a protest against the exclusiveness of the Jews, and insisting that God cares for all people, Gentiles as well as Jews. (The entire Book of Jonah is today read in synagogues on the Day of Atonement, or Yom Kippur.)

What happened to Jonah when he was thrown into the sea?

The reason why Jonah, in the famous story, was on board a ship in the first place was that he was trying to get away from God (Yahweh), who had ordered him to go to Nineveh, much against his wishes. There was a great storm and the sailors were afraid. The sailors threw Jonah overboard regretfully, on his own advice, because he supposed that Yahweh was making the sea rough in order to wreck the ship and drown Jonah. However, God arranged for him to be saved by being swallowed by "a great fish" (the text does not say it was a whale), which later coughed him up on land.

A frustrated Jonah in his shelter, or "booth," where God taught him to be tolerant of Gentiles.

Where was Nineveh?

Nineveh was the last capital of the Assyrian empire, on the Tigris River in Mesopotamia. Among its ruins, which have been investigated by archeologists, there are several large mounds, one of which is known as the Tomb of Jonah.

Nineveh was a great city, with grand royal palaces and a population of over 100,000 people—a great number 2,500 years ago. There, archeologists have also discovered a huge library of clay tablets in the palace of Assurbanipal and, among other art treasures, stone carvings of Assyrian military campaigns and an account of the siege of Jerusalem.

At the time the Book of Jonah was written, Nineveh was, for the Jews, a symbol of Gentile paganism. It was because of this that Jonah was unwilling to obey God and preach there.

What happened to Jonah's shelter? Jonah 4

To Jonah's surprise, the people of Nineveh repented when they heard his message and, as a result, God did not carry out his threat to destroy the city. This made Jonah angry, because his prophecy had proved to be wrong, and he went out of the city and built himself a shelter, where he sat sulking. God caused a climbing plant to grow up and shade him from the sun, but the next day the plant was attacked by parasites and withered away. This made Jonah even angrier.

But then God asked: if Jonah was sorry for the plant, why should God not be sorry for the the great city of Nineveh?

The point of the story is probably that Israel (represented by Jonah) should show more sympathy to the Gentiles (Nineveh).

What does "Apocalypse" mean?

"Apocalypse" means "revelation," a prophecy revealing the word of God directly. The most famous example is the Revelation of St John the Divine in the New Testament (and the modern usage of "apocalypse" to mean a violent event refers to such events in Revelation). Apocalyptic literature became common toward the end of the period covered by the Old Testament, and it encouraged the hope for a Messiah. The apocalyptic style appears in many of the books of the Prophets, including Isaiah, and became fully established in the Book of Daniel.

When was the Book of Daniel written?

The Prophet Daniel, about whom nothing is known except for the stories in the Book of Daniel, was supposedly one of the captives in Babylon during the exile in the 6th century BC. However, it seems likely that the Book was actually composed in about 165 BC, which makes it probably the last of the Books of the Old Testament to be written. That was a time of dreadful persecution of the Jews by the Seleucid emperor Antiochus Epiphanes, and the Book of Daniel contains an attack on him and his court, disguised as Nebuchadnezzar and the Babylonians.

The Book of Daniel is an apocalypse, pointing to a future golden age of the spirit, with mysteries and miracles, supernatural wonders, strange symbols and people. The Prophets had forecast a golden age which would follow the return from Babylon, but this had not occurred. Apolyptic writings were partly a response to this disappointment.

Why did Nebuchadnezzar threaten to kill his wisest advisers? Daniel 2

King Nebuchadnezzar was much troubled by dreams, and spent many a restless night. After one particular dream which upset him greatly, he summoned his wisest advisers in the hope that they could explain what the dream meant. But, as a test of their powers, Nebuchadnezzar insisted that they should tell him what the dream had been, as well as what it meant. Naturally, they could not do that, and Nebuchadnezzar, flying into a rage, ordered all the wise men in the kingdom to be put to death.

Daniel fell into this category, but when he discovered why such a dreadful decree had been issued, he asked for a little time to consider, then went to Nebuchadnezzar and told him both his dream and its meaning, thus saving a lot of wise men from execution.

A visitor touches the mezuzah outside the door of a house. It serves as a reminder of religious duty.

What is a mezuzah?

On the doorpost of a house belonging to very religious Jews you will see a small case made of wood or metal. It contains a small parchment on which is written certain verses from the Book of Deuteronomy, Chapter 6, verses 4 to 9 ("Hear, O Israel: The Lord our God is one Lord, And thou shalt love the Lord thy God with all thine heart") and Chapter 11, verses 13 to 21, with, on the other side, one of the names used to signify God. The purpose of the mezuzah is to remind people of their religious duty, and the custom can perhaps be traced back to the time when the Israelites were trying to escape from Egypt, and marked their doors so that the angel of God would pass them by on his errand of destruction.

How did Daniel interpret Nebuchadnezzar's dream?

Daniel alone was able to tell Nebuchadnezzar his dream. He told the king he had dreamed of a huge figure, made of gold, silver, bronze and iron, with feet half of iron and half of clay. The statue was shattered by a great stone cut from a mountain, though not by human hands. It crashed to the ground in fragments so small that they were blown away by the wind. But the stone grew into a great mountain, filling all the world.

The meaning of the dream Daniel explained like this. The various metals making up the huge figure stood for different empires which would rule the world (the fifth empire, made partly of iron and partly of clay, would be part strong and part weak). The great stone which shattered the figure and grew into a mountain that filled the world was the final empire—the empire of God.

What were the four empires in Nebuchadnezzar's dream?

The king had dreamed of a gigantic figure with a head of gold, body of silver, belly and thighs of bronze, legs of iron, and feet half clay and half iron. According to Daniel, they represented earthly empires. The gold head was the current empire—the empire of the Babylonians; the silver (and therefore slightly inferior) empire was the empire of the Medes, bronze the Persians, iron the empire of Alexander the Great, and the weakest—the mixture of iron and clay—was the divided empire of the Ptolemies and the Seleucids which followed Alexander. At least, this was the interpretation put on them by Daniel. However, the history is not quite right because there was no empire of the Medes between the Babylonians and the Persians.

Who were Shadrach, Meshach and Abednego? Daniel 3

When Daniel was made governor of Babylonia by Nebuchadnezzar, the Prophet asked for three of his associates—Shadrach, Meshach, and Abednego—to serve under him. They were, of course, devout Jews like Daniel himself (though they have Babylonian names), and when Nebuchadnezzar set up a great gold statue and commanded his subjects to worship it, they would not do so. The punishment was to be thrown into a burning, fiery furnace. But when Shadrach, Meshach and Abednego were thrown into the furnace, the flames did not touch them, and they walked through the fire without feeling the heat. Nebuchadnezzar was so impressed that he ordered them to be restored to their posts in the government.

Daniel himself is not mentioned in this story, which probably comes from another source. The purpose of the story was to encourage the Jews to remain true to their faith and not bow down to false gods.

What happened at Belshazzar's feast? Daniel 5

Belshazzar, who is described as Nebuchadnezzar's son and successor although this is an historical error, was giving a feast and used the sacred vessels from the Temple at Jerusalem. They praised their own gods—graven images in stone or metal. Suddenly, a disembodied hand appeared and wrote a mysterious message on the wall. At the Queen's suggestion, Daniel, now an old man, was summoned to interpret it. Belshazzar promised him a vast reward if he could tell the meaning of the words.

The words written on the wall were *Mene, mene, tekel, u-pharsin*. Scholars have puzzled over them at great length, and it seems that they could have at least three meanings. However, the only one that really matters is the explanation given by Daniel.

Mene means "numbered," and Belshazzar's days were numbered because he had been "measured"—*tekel* is a weight—and found wanting (since he worshiped false gods and committed sacrilege). Therefore, his kingdom would be "divided"—the probable meaning of *u-pharsin*—between the Medes and Persians.

The same night, according to the Book of Daniel, the Medes captured the city. They killed Belshazzar and so ended the empire of Babylonia. Daniel survived and was honored by the new rulers.

Q What was Daniel's reward for interpreting the message on the wall? Daniel 5

A The interpretation given by Daniel of the mysterious words written on the palace wall by the disembodied hand was a very gloomy one as far as Belshazzar was concerned. Nevertheless, Daniel was richly rewarded. Although he told the king to keep his presents, which were of no interest to him, he was nevertheless robed in purple, a gold chain was hung around his neck, and he was made the third most important person in the kingdom.

Daniel in the lions' den

Who were the Medes and the Persians?

The Medes and the Persians were separate, though related, peoples who came from what is now Iran. The kingdom of the Medes reached its height about the time of Nebuchadnezzar, when they controlled a large area roughly to the north of the Babylonian empire. The Persians, a smaller nation, were then generally under the dominance of the Medes.

However, when Cyrus the Great became king of the Persians in the 6th century BC, he united the two peoples, and thereafter "the Medes and the Persians," as the Bible refers to them, were, in effect, one people. Cyrus went on to overthrow Babylon in 539, and allowed the Jews to return to Palestine. The Persian empire remained the greatest power in the world until it was smashed by Alexander the Great in the 4th century BC.

How was Daniel tricked into breaking the law? Daniel 6

Daniel, who had been so highly regarded by the kings of Babylon, was also favored by their Persian successors. The Persian king Darius made him one of his chief ministers, and planned to make him the governor of Babylonia. Not surprisingly, this irritated Darius's Persian officials, and they set out to ruin Daniel.

They did not find it easy, because Daniel was a just and careful minister. His one weak point, they thought, was his religion. They went to the king and suggested that he should make a law forbidding people to ask for anything from any god or man, except from the king himself. Darius agreed to this rather strange request.

Daniel, a devout man, prayed three times a day. He had windows made in his house so he could face toward Jerusalem when he was praying. This made it easy for spies to catch him in the act. They went to Darius and accused Daniel of breaking the new law because he was praying to his God. The king now realized that the whole thing was a trick, but there was a strict rule that the law of the Medes could not be changed. So Daniel had to suffer the penalty—to be thrown to the lions.

What happened in the lions' den?

Darius was forced to obey his own law, although against his will, and ordered Daniel to be placed in the lions' den. He had some hope that Daniel's God, to whom his minister was so faithful, would save him.

Daniel was lowered into the pit where the hungry lions prowled, and a great stone was put over the top so that he could not escape or be rescued. Darius spent a sleepless night and, at dawn, hurried to the pit, fearing the worst. He had the stone hauled away and called down into the darkness, "Daniel! Has your God preserved you?" To his great delight, Daniel's voice replied, "Long life to you, King Darius! God sent his angels to prevent the lions hurting me, because I have done no wrong to them— or to you!"

Daniel was lifted from the pit, and those who had accused him were lowered down in his place. The lions at once tore them to pieces.

The Jews did not have special buildings for worship until the idea of the synagogue took hold.

Where were the first synagogues?

A synagogue, like a church, is a place for prayer and worship, but it is also used for instruction, especially in the Jewish Law. And as well as being a school, it is a social center, where local affairs are discussed.

Synagogues are not mentioned in the Old Testament, though by Jesus's time they were to be found in every town. There were dozens in Jerusalem alone.

No one can say for certain how synagogues began, but it is obvious that they grew up very rapidly after the Jews' return from exile, and therefore it must have been in Babylon that they began. There, people could no longer go to the Temple, so they took to meeting in private houses for prayer, singing and discussion. We know they gathered in the house of the Prophet Ezekiel, and this may have been the beginnings of the synagogue.

Who allowed the Jews to go home?

Cyrus the Great, founder of the Persian empire, was not only a great conqueror, he was also a ruler well known for his tolerance. He was usually kind to the people he conquered, and he did not destroy them because of their beliefs. After he had captured Babylon, he issued an edict, or decree, saying that the Hebrew people could return to the land of their fathers and rebuild their Temple in Jerusalem.

Not surprisingly, Old Testament writers speak well of Cyrus. In the Book of Isaiah, he is called God's shepherd. Some people have suggested that he may have been converted to the worship of the Hebrew God, but the Bible does not say so and it seems unlikely.

How did farmers plow their fields?

The life of farming people did not change very quickly in ancient times, and in fact you might still see a plow like those used in Old Testament times in some parts of the Middle East today.

The plow was really no more than a pointed stick. It did not have a plowshare, or blade, like modern plows, and it scratched a deep groove in the ground rather than cutting and turning it in a slice. The plow was made of wood, although the tip was of metal, and it had a handle attached to the shaft, so that the man plowing could hold the point down. He had to lean quite hard on it, otherwise it would bounce over the ground instead of cutting into

The plow of Old Testament times was a simple tool which, in effect, hoed the ground rather than dug it.

it. The plow was dragged by two oxen, (in early times, perhaps by donkeys), or by just one animal. The far end was attached to a yoke, tied to the necks of the ox or oxen.

The time to plow was late October and early November, when the winter rains had started, softening the ground, and the seed was soon to be sown.

Grapes, to be turned into wine, were crushed by the simple method of treading.

Q **Why were watchtowers built in the fields?**

A Watchtowers were built at certain places, such as crossroads or gates in a city wall, so that sentries could be sheltered from attack and give warning of enemies.

Smaller watchtowers were also built in vineyards and fields. They were leaf-covered shelters, or booths, which were placed, if possible, in the highest part of the field to avoid having to build a tower. Members of the farmer's family would keep watch on the growing crop all through the season—chiefly against animals or other pests. It seems that sometimes the watchtowers in the fields were occupied by proper guards, who could probably keep an eye on a great many fields from their tower.

Who were the Samaritans?

The district of Samaria is in the center of Palestine. During the period of the two kingdoms, the chief city—also called Samaria—was the capital of Israel, the northern kingdom. It was a richer country than Judah to the south, and better suited for growing crops.

When the Hebrew inhabitants were driven into exile by the Assyrians in the 8th century BC, a variety of other peoples were placed in Samaria. The Samaritans therefore became a mixed race of people: partly Jewish, partly Babylonian, and partly other races. As well as not being "pure" in race, the Samaritans were also not "pure" in religion, and because of this, they were despised by the Jews.

Who led the Jews back to Jerusalem?

When Cyrus, the Persian king, told the Jews in Babylon that they could go home, not all of them did so. A large number remained in Babylon, although some groups later trickled back to Palestine. Cyrus appointed a governor of Jerusalem named Sheshbazzar to lead the exiles home again.

According to another tradition, Zerubbabel, a descendant of King David, was the leader of the exiles returning from Babylon. It is possible that Sheshbazzar and Zerubbabel were actually the same man. If not, Sheshbazzar must have left the city soon after the exiles returned.

Why did rebuilding the Temple prove so difficult?

The first task of the Jews who returned from exile in Babylon was to rebuild the Temple. In their homeland now, however, they were surrounded by people whom they regarded as foreigners—Samaritans and others. Although the Samaritans worshiped Yahweh, their style of worship was different, and they worshiped other gods, too. The Jews, who had learned to guard their own beliefs and customs closely while they were in exile, wanted nothing to do with the Samaritans and, as a result, when the latter wanted to take part in the great task of rebuilding the Temple, the Jews refused.

Then the Samaritans made things so difficult for the builders that they gave up, telling themselves that God did not want the Temple to be rebuilt—at least, not yet. But times were hard, and the Prophets Haggai and Zechariah warned that they would get no better until the reconstruction of the Temple was complete. Also, news came from Persia that the Persian king had ordered that the Temple should be rebuilt. So the builders began again, and although they were still opposed by the Samaritans, the job was finished in four years.

Why did old people cry when they saw the foundations of the new Temple? Ezra 3

When the builders had laid the foundations of the new Temple, after the return of the exiles from Babylon, there was naturally a great celebration. But, as the Book of Ezra reports, some people wept and wailed, although it was hard to hear their cries of distress among the shouts of joy. Those who cried were the older people, who remembered the old Temple which had been destroyed.

Scholars have decided that this means the new Temple must have been a much smaller building, although it seems possible that it was just the sad memories of destruction which made the old people cry.

What building stands on the site of the Temple today?

Jerusalem is a holy city in three religions—Judaism, Christianity, and Islam.

There were really three Temples in Jerusalem. The first, Solomon's Temple, was destroyed by the Babylonians. The second, less grand, was built after the return of the Jews from the Babylonian Captivity. This temple was destroyed by soldiers of the Seleucid emperor Antiochus Epiphanes in the 2nd century BC. The third and biggest Temple—the Temple of the New Testament—was built about 15 years before Jesus's birth and destroyed in AD 70.

Today, the building which stands on the site of the Temple is the magnificent Muslim mosque known as the Dome of the Rock. This covers the rock from which it is said the Prophet Muhammad, the founder of Islam, rose into heaven.

Who rebuilt Jerusalem? Nehemiah 2

The Babylonian exiles returned to a ruined city, with weeds growing everywhere. The first task after the rebuilding of the Temple was to restore Jerusalem itself.

For many years, the houses and walls of the city remained in ruins. News of this sad state of affairs came to Nehemiah, a Jew who had risen high in the service of the Persian king. It made him so sad that the king noticed it and asked him what the matter was. Nehemiah replied that he was grieving for the state of Jerusalem, and when the king gave a sympathetic answer, he asked him if he might go there to rebuild it. The king gave permission, and provided him with letters of authority to get the building materials which would be needed.

Nehemiah's commission was greeted with enthusiasm by the Jews in Jerusalem, but there was a lot of opposition from the foreigners living there. Nehemiah had to divide his work force into two groups: one to rebuild the walls, while the other acted as guards against attack from the opponents of the Jews. Once the walls had been rebuilt, work on the buildings could continue in peace.

Rebuilding the walls of Jerusalem after the Exile. The city, which was to be destroyed again several times, had a troubled history. But in later times it always held a powerful attraction for Jews scattered throughout the world.

How did the Jews celebrate the rebuilding of Jerusalem? Nehemiah 8

Like the re-building of the Temple, the re-building of the walls of Jerusalem was celebrated with singing and dancing. Two great choirs walked in procession around them, in opposite directions, afterward coming together in the Temple to attend a sacrifice. The Law was read, and it was at this time that the people rediscovered the Feast of Tabernacles, or Booths (the simple huts made of branches which were put up by farmers in the fields—and by Jonah when he left Nineveh). This Feast was originally a harvest festival, but it also commemorated the time when the whole nation had lived in booths after the Exodus from Egypt. The booths for the festival were put up on the roofs of houses, and the feasting lasted for eight days.

What were houses like in Old Testament times?

The houses of ordinary people in Palestine were small, single-story, squarish buildings with flat roofs. In that hot, dry climate, the roof was an important part of the house, and was reached by an outside staircase. The walls were brick, plastered on the inside, and there was really only a single room, with a floor of hard, baked mud.

The room was divided in two by steps, one

This type of house built in Biblical times can still be seen in parts of the Middle East.

half of the room being on a lower level. In this lower part lived the family's animals—a donkey, one or two goats, perhaps an ox. However, the animals spent a good deal of time outside, when the lower part could be used for weaving or other crafts. In the family's section, there was a fireplace in the middle of the room, but no chimney. Smoke went out through the windows, which had no glass. They were rather small and set high in the walls. In that climate, the sunlight is best kept out, not let in.

What happened to Tobiah's belongings? Nehemiah 13

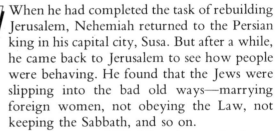

When he had completed the task of rebuilding Jerusalem, Nehemiah returned to the Persian king in his capital city, Susa. But after a while, he came back to Jerusalem to see how people were behaving. He found that the Jews were slipping into the bad old ways—marrying foreign women, not obeying the Law, not keeping the Sabbath, and so on.

A priest named Eliashib, who was in charge of the Temple storerooms, had given a room in the Temple precincts to Tobiah, who was a relative of his by marriage. Nehemiah was so angry at this sacrilege that he threw all of Tobiah's belongings out of the room.

Why did the Jews reject all foreigners? Ezra 9

Perhaps the most astonishing thing about the Jews throughout history is that, although they were a very small nation and usually at the mercy of stronger powers, they kept their religion and their way of life (which was almost the same thing) alive and healthy. This was done at a cost, however.

When the Prophet Ezra (who, with Nehemiah, was the person most responsible for the restoration of Israel after the Babylonian Captivity) came to Jerusalem, he was told that many of the people, and especially the leading men who should have shown an example, had married foreign wives.

When he heard this, Ezra tore his robe in anger and despair, he tore at his hair and beard and, he said, he sat on the ground, completely dumbfounded. He prayed, and weeping, confessed to God that the nation had done wrong. This was a very serious matter—although it is hard for us to realize just how serious. The worst thing about it was that it would lead to the worship of false gods, against which the Prophets and others had waged such a great battle since the days of Moses.

The reforms of Nehemiah and Ezra were effective in the end. The Jews kept their religon "pure" and strict for a long time—until the coming of Jesus. However, by that time, their concern for the Law had become dry, rigid, and unfeeling. The strict letter of the Law had become more important than justice, or humanity, or plain common sense. That was the reason later for Jesus's fierce attacks on the Pharisees.

Crushing olives in a press, in which a donkey moves the stone "wheel."

What was olive oil used for?

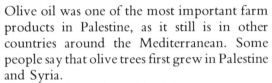

Olive oil was one of the most important farm products in Palestine, as it still is in other countries around the Mediterranean. Some people say that olive trees first grew in Palestine and Syria.

Olive oil was the only oil there was, except for some precious scents which were in the form of oil. It was used for a great many purposes, even, at one time, as a means of exchange—instead of money. Solomon paid some of the costs of building the Temple in olive oil.

Its chief use was in cooking, mainly frying and seasoning. Butter was a luxury, and olive oil was often used instead. Otherwise, the main use of olive oil in ordinary life was in lamps. But it was also used for anointing a king, soothing feet, putting on bruises and minor injuries and for other purposes.

How was olive oil obtained?

When the olives were ripe, they were knocked off the trees with a long stick. This is not really a good method as it harms the tree and may stop it bearing fruit the next season, but the Israelites were not too concerned about this because olive trees were so common. The olives were then pounded with a mortar and pestle—a

heavy basin and a blunt-ended club—until the oil could be poured off.

A better method was to use an olive press, if you had one. A simple form of olive press consisted of a very large stone shaped like a thick wheel (a section of a stone pillar was sometimes used) with a pole sticking out of the middle. A man (or woman) turned the wheel inside a broad basin containing the olives. The olives were crushed to pulp, which was mixed with hot water and then further pressed with a heavy beam—or with bare feet, as in winemaking. Afterward, the oil had to stand in jars for some time to settle.

What was the message of the Prophet Micah?

The Prophet Micah lived in Judah in the 8th century BC, and his Book was written during his lifetime, though it seems to have been altered after his death. He was a countryman with a strong sense of justice and an equally strong distrust of townspeople, landowners, government officials, and priests.

Micah saw the threat of the Assyrians as the hand of God, about to punish Israel. Micah's message was simple: Listen to God's word; act justly; be kind and loving; walk humbly with God.

Micah also prophesied that after a long period of disaster, peace would come again, and Israel would produce a Messiah, who would be a great leader, like King David.

How was wine made?

 Palestine is a good country for growing grapes, and in Old Testament days, the grape harvest was a joyful time. The ripe grapes were carried in carts and baskets to the wine press. This was a stone tank, sometimes cut out of the solid rock. It had a hole near the bottom through which the juice could flow to a smaller container. The juice was squeezed from the grapes by people trampling them with their bare feet. They hung on to ropes over their heads as they trampled, and sang songs.

The grape juice was stored in clay jars, or in skins: the whole skin of a goat, with the feet tied to prevent leaks, made a good container. The juice fermented in the skin bags or jars, which means it turned into wine. It could not be drunk right away; it was ready about 40 days later. It could then be strained and drunk, although it was better if left longer.

 ## What is the Apocrypha?

All Christian Bibles have two major sections, the Old Testament and the New Testament. But some Bibles—those of the Roman Catholic, Episcopalian (Anglican) and Greek Orthodox Churches—contain another section between the Old and New Testaments. This is the Apocrypha.

The other Protestant denominations say that the Apocrypha is non-canonical, which means it does not have the divine authority of the rest of the Bible. Martin Luther, the leading figure of the Protestant Reformation in the 16th century, described the Apocrypha as "books which are not equal to the sacred Scriptures, and yet are useful and good for reading." However, there is no general agreement.

The books of the Apocrypha are especially important for giving us information about the history of Palestine and the Jews during the period between the end of the Old Testament and the beginning of the New Testament.

The books include: 1 and 2 Esdras, Tobit, Judith, Additions to Daniel, Susanna, Bel and the Dragon, Additions to Esther, prayer of Manasses, Book of Baruch, Ecclesiasticus, The Wisdom of Solomon, 1 and 2 Maccabees, Song of the 3 Holy Children.

 ## How was the Old Testament written?

 The Old Testament was written over a very long period of time—more than 1,000 years. Most of the actual writing-down was done in Palestine or Babylon (during the Exile). A lot of the Old Testament was written centuries after the events being described. Stories were passed down by word of mouth, from parent to child, for many years. For example, the Israelites' Exodus from Egypt happened in about 1300 BC, but the Book of Exodus was written about 900 BC. Probably the oldest parts of the Old Testament are certain poems, like the Song of Deborah in Chapter 5 of the Book of Judges.

Few Books of the Old Testament, as we know them, are exactly the same as they were when they were first written. The texts on which our Bible is based were not, of course, the earliest texts, all of which have vanished. The writers, in any case, often used several different documents, or sources.

 ## Who wrote the Book of Ecclesiasticus?

The Book of Ecclesiasticus is the seventh Book of the Apocrypha. We know more about the writer then we do about almost any other writer of Old Testament scriptures. His name was Jesus (or Joshua) Ben Sira, a teacher in Jerusalem who was influenced by Greek ideas. Like the Greeks, he thought that knowledge was a good thing, and that a good man was a learned man, just as the Hebrews believed that a godly man was a law-abiding man. His book is full of good advice on all sorts of subjects, from death to drinking.

The Book of Jesus Ben Sira was known only in a Greek translation until the last century, when large parts of the original Hebrew version were discovered.

 ## Who was Alexander the Great?

 Alexander was the great conqueror who, in the late 4th century BC, conquered the Persian empire and established his own, which stretched from Greece to India and included most of what was then known of the civilized world.

Alexander was a very remarkable person, but more important was the effect of his amazing conquests, which brought to the ancient Near East, where all the leading centers of civilization had been for thousands of years, the influence of Greek ideas. Greek life and thought was in many ways quite different from that of the older civilizations of Persia, Mesopotamia and Egypt. A powerful influence, it brought many changes and caused many conflicts, not least among the Jews.

How did the Jews become Hellenized?

Hellenized means "Greekified," and it refers to the spread of Greek or Hellenistic influence which followed the conquests of Alexander the Great.

Palestine became part of Alexander's empire. This was no great hardship, as the Jews were allowed to continue with their own laws and religion. However, many Jews, especially younger people, were strongly influenced by Greek ideas. Although Greek religion was not a very powerful attraction—it had none of the strength of Judaism—in other ways, Greek customs and ideas were very attractive. This caused trouble, although it was quite possible to accept Greek influences and still remain a good Jew like Ben Sira, the author of the Book of Ecclesiasticus, and members of the political party known as the Sadducees.

What did the Sadducees believe?

No one knows how the Sadducees got their name. It may have come from the name of Zadok, the priest who anointed Solomon as king. The Sadducees originated with a group of well-educated, intelligent Hellenized Jews like Ben Sira, author of the Book of Ecclesiasticus. They represented the upper-class, priestly types in Jerusalem, and considered that there was great value in learning, social status and worldly power. They did not believe in life after death, nor in angels or spirits. In many ways, their ideas were directly opposed to the Pharisees.

The Sadducees were a small political party, but they had great influence. Many of them were members of the Sanhedrin, the supreme court of the Jews. They were not very popular with the people, with whom they did not mix. That is one reason why the Sadducees were denounced by Jesus.

The Sadducees were the "cream" of society in the two centuries before Jesus.

What crops did farmers grow?

Farming was the main occupation of the people of ancient Palestine. The crops that were grown varied according to the region: crops which grew well in the Jordan valley would not do so well on the hills. In nearly all parts, drought was a frequent danger.

The biggest grain crops were wheat and barley, and the next most important were olives and grapes. Grain, oil and wine—these were the basic products, and they are often mentioned together in the Bible.

Other crops were mostly grown in a smaller scale, and in any case, most farms were small. Beans and lentils were grown widely, and cucumbers are often mentioned in the Bible. Herbs such as dill (still a great Jewish favorite) would be grown near the house, and there was also fruit, especially figs (the trees of which gave a pleasant shade), pomegranates, dates and nuts such as almonds.

Who were the Seleucids?

After the death of Alexander the Great in 323 BC, his empire was split up as various generals and governors fought among themselves. Eventually, two empires were formed: that of the Ptolemies, whose main base was Egypt, and that of the Seleucids, whose center of power was Mesopotamia. Palestine was more or less in the middle, between these two great powers. The Ptolemies ruled it at first, but later it fell to the Seleucids, who already held Syria. Under their rule, Judea became more fully Hellenized, and this caused a Jewish rebellion under the leadership of the Maccabees, which began in 167 BC.

What happened in the reign of Antiochus Epiphanes?

This Seleucid emperor, who reigned from 175 to 164 BC, is one of the great villains in Jewish history. He was eager to unify his empire, and one way of doing this was to make sure that there was only one religion throughout his lands. That meant stamping out Judaism altogether. Antiochus, who had already stripped the Temple of its gold ornaments to pay for his wars, had an altar to the Greek god Zeus erected in the Temple. He believed—or he acted as though he believed—that he was a god himself. The ancient Hebrew Law was suppressed and all the old customs were forbidden on pain of death.

The policy of Hellenization, which Antiochus enforced so brutally, was accepted by many Jews. This caused a deep split between orthodox religious Jews and Hellenized Jews who were quite willing to worship at pagan altars.

Who were the Maccabees?

The efforts of Antiochus Epiphanes to stamp out the Jewish religion and the Jewish way of life caused a rebellion. It began in 167 BC when a man named Mattathias killed an official who had come to the town of Modein to make the people sacrifice to pagan gods. Together with his five sons, Mattathias fled into the hills. Others joined them, and when Mattathias died the following year, one of his sons, Judas Maccabeus, "The Hammer," became leader of the revolt.

What began as the desperate acts of a small band of guerrilla fighters soon became a great national rebellion. Jerusalem was recaptured and the Temple purified. All Jews were forced to keep the Law of Moses.

The struggle continued for many years. All five of Mattathias's sons died by violence. But they did not die in vain: in 142 BC the Seleucid rulers were forced to accept Jewish independence.

How long did the Jews keep their independence?

After the Seleucids had recognized Jewish independence in 142 BC, the Maccabeus family became the hereditary holders of the office of high priest as well as rulers of the kingdom. They were a warlike line, and conquered many of their neighbors, forcing them to accept Judaism.

They were not popular with all Jews either, especially with the Pharisees. Under Alexander

Jannaeus (103–78 BC), there was civil war which lasted for six years.

The Seleucid empire, which had already been growing weaker at the time of the Maccabean rebellion nearly a century earlier, had long since fallen apart. It was partly the absence of a great power in the Middle East which allowed an independent Jewish kingdom to exist for so long. However, there was a great and growing power to the west—Rome—and Roman ambitions were growing. In 63 BC, the Roman general Pompey captured Jerusalem, and Jewish independence was at an end.

A reconstruction of the Temple of Jupiter, on the Capitoline Hill, the most famous of the seven hills of Rome. It was here that victorious generals would go to offer thanks.

Can we learn more about ancient Israel?

Much of our knowledge of ancient Palestine depends on the Bible, and the Bible has been with us for many centuries. But in the past 200 years we have learned a great deal more about ancient places and peoples through archeology. If you can find a copy of an atlas of the Bible published about 50 or 60 years ago and compare it with a modern one, you will be able to see at a glance how archeologists have discovered much more about the Bible lands. Nearly all the main places mentioned in the Bible are now known, and there have been archeological "digs" at many of them. (Of course, this is not so easy in a place that is still a city today, such as Jerusalem or Damascus.)

Our knowledge of ancient Palestine has probably grown more in the past 100 years than in the 1,000 years before that. And it will keep on growing.

What is the Septuagint?

The Septuagint is the translation of the Old Testament into Greek. Most of the Old Testament was, of course, written in Hebrew, and the Greek version was made for the many Greek-speaking Jews in the 3rd century BC. It was produced by a group of scholars working, probably, in Alexandria, in Egypt.

It was probably the best-known version of the Old Testament scriptures in the time of Jesus, because when New Testament writers referred to the Old Testament, they usually quoted from the Septuagint.

 Who were the Essenes?

The Essenes were a strict religious sect or "order" among the Jews, founded in the 2nd century BC. They lived in communities, like monks. One was in Qumran by the Dead Sea. They spent most of their time praying and studying the Law. Like the early Christians,

they had no private property. They are not so well known as other religious orders, such as the Sadducees and the Pharisees, because they had nothing to do with ordinary affairs and kept themselves apart. They are not often mentioned in the Bible.

The Essenes thought of themselves as the heirs of the earliest Israelites who had wandered

112

Q What are the Dead Sea Scrolls?

A By far the greatest discovery in Bible studies for hundreds of years began in 1947, when a young Bedouin shepherd found clay jars which contained ancient manuscripts in a cave near the Dead Sea. Later, many more manuscripts were found in other caves nearby—some found by archeologists but rather more by Bedouin.

The Dead Sea Scrolls contain, apart from other writings, portions of almost every book in the Old Testament, written in Hebrew or Aramaic. These manuscripts are, in most cases, centuries older than the oldest Hebrew versions of the Scriptures that were known at the time of the discovery. Such a find was indeed a miracle.

Even today, the study of the Dead Sea Scrolls is at an early stage—there is still so much to do. One comforting thing we have learned

The discovery of the Dead Sea Scrolls in caves near the Dead Sea was the greatest event for Biblical studies in centuries.

in the desert in the time of Moses. They expected the coming of a new age, in which the world would be swept clean of all the sin and corruption they saw around them. The Essenes are especially important to us because they were the authors, or guardians, of the Dead Sea Scrolls. You will see in the next question just how important these were.

so far is that our version of the Scriptures seems to be very faithful to the original: some of the Dead Sea manuscripts are almost exactly the same, and they are very close to the Septuagint.

The Scrolls were probably hidden about AD 68, at the time of the Jewish revolt against Roman rule. They are the remains of a large library belonging to the Essenes of Qumran.

The New Testament

What are the Gospels?

The word "gospel" means "good news." The good news is God's action in sending his Son to Earth for the salvation of human beings. The story of Jesus's mission is told in the first four books of the New Testament, and these books are therefore called the Gospels.

The early Christian Church only knew about Jesus from what the Apostles and others had to say. This knowledge all depended on the spoken word—nothing was written down. It was to meet the overwhelming need for a permanent record of the story of Jesus that the Gospels were written.

Do the Gospels all tell the same story?

The four Gospels are different books, although there is a close resemblance between the first three Gospels—Matthew, Mark, and Luke. The fourth, John, is quite different.

Mark, the shortest Gospel, was also probably the earliest. It says nothing about Jesus's early life—nothing, for instance, about the Nativity, the Christmas story. This is told in only two Gospels (Matthew and Luke), and many of the best-loved details of that story are told only in Luke.

The four Gospel writers had slightly different ideas about Jesus. Matthew shows him as, above all, the Messiah promised by the Prophets of the Old Testament; he was probably writing for Jewish Christians. Mark is most interested in Jesus as a worker of wonderful deeds. Luke's Gospel seems to be written mainly for Christians of non-Jewish origin. John has very little in common with the others, and it contains many details—for example, about the Resurrection—which they do not mention.

What is a codex?

When the Bible talks about a book, it actually means a scroll—a long piece of parchment or papyrus which is unrolled as it is read. (Parchment is made from animal skin, and papyrus is a kind of paper made from papyrus reeds.)

The scroll was later replaced by something more like a book, which is called a "codex" (the plural is "codices"). Several sheets of papyrus were put together, folded in half, and then stitched along the fold. Scrolls were still used by the Jews in Jesus's day and for some time afterward. But most of the earliest versions of the Scriptures, which date from the 4th–5th centuries AD, are in the form of codices.

The earliest writings were on tablets of clay or wax. When parchment, and later papyrus, came into use, it was made in the form of rolls, which were unwound as they were read.

116

Who were the parents of John the Baptist? Luke 1

John the Baptist was born before Jesus and prepared the way for him. His mother, Elizabeth, was a cousin of Mary, mother of Jesus, so the two were related.

Elizabeth was married to a priest of the Temple named Zachariah. They had no children, and Elizabeth was past the age when, usually, women can have children. But one day, when Zachariah was in the Holy Place in the Temple, burning incense at the altar, an angel appeared and told him that Elizabeth would have a son, who should be called John. He would prepare the people for the coming of the Lord. Zachariah was doubtful, because of his wife's age. The angel said that Zachariah would not be able to speak until the day of the child's birth, because he had doubted the word of God's messenger.

What messages did Gabriel bring? Luke 1

The archangel Gabriel was God's messenger. He appeared in the Temple to tell Zachariah of the coming birth of his son—John the Baptist—and six months later he visited Nazareth. He appeared to a young woman called Mary, who was engaged to be married to Joseph, a descendant of King David. Mary was naturally afraid of this strange vision, but Gabriel told her to have no fear. She was to have a son, whom she must call Jesus. He would be the son of the Most High, and God would give him the throne of David. He would reign for ever.

Mary asked how this was possible. The angel said, "The Holy Spirit will come upon you. Your son will be holy and will be called the Son of God."

What is the Annunciation? Luke 1

The word "annunciation" means "announcement." It is the name given to the visit of the angel Gabriel to Mary at Nazareth, when he announced the coming birth of Jesus. A Christian festival of the Annunciation commemorates that event on 25 March, which is some-

times known as Lady Day. There is an old tradition that this is a good day to sow seeds: if planted on Lady Day, plants will do well.

Who was Gabriel?

The Hebrew name Gabriel means "man of God." He was the heavenly messenger who announced the forthcoming birth of, first, John the Baptist, and, second, Jesus. He was also the messenger sent to Daniel to explain the meaning of his dream of the fight between a ram and a goat (Daniel 8).

Gabriel explained to Zachariah that he was one of God's attendants, and he is therefore called an archangel—that is, a superior angel (just as an archbishop is a superior bishop). There were said to be either seven or four archangels. In the ancient Hebrew writings called the Books of Enoch (not in the Bible), the other three archangels are named as Michael, Uriel and Suriel or Raphael. Besides Gabriel, Michael is the best known. He was the special guardian of Israel.

The figure of Gabriel was taken over by Islam. He is mentioned several times in the Koran, though not always by name, and is the same kind of figure as he is in the Bible.

Who named John the Baptist? Luke 1

Not long after the Annunciation, Mary's cousin Elizabeth gave birth to a son, as the angel Gabriel had prophesied. Elizabeth said the child would be called John. This surprised her relatives, because there was no one called John in the family, and boys were usually named after their grandfather or father. They asked Zachariah what he wanted the baby to be called. He was still unable to speak, but they gave him a clay tablet to write on, and he wrote, "His name is John." At that moment, speech returned to him.

What made this such an impressive story to those who heard it was that *both* parents said the child's name was to be John. Gabriel had only told Zachariah that this was his name, and since then, Zachariah had been unable to speak. Yet Elizabeth too chose the name John.

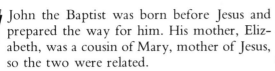
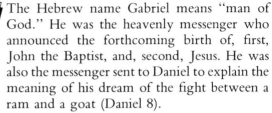
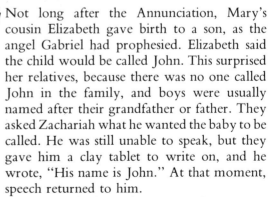

Who was the Messiah?

"Messiah" is the Hebrew form of "the Christ," and means "the Anointed One," the "Deliverer" or "Saviour." There was an ancient tradition among the Jews that God would send a Messiah to deliver them from their enemies and establish the Kingdom of God. After the return from Exile, when the Jews went through many bad times, this idea grew still stronger.

It was not clear what kind of kingdom the "Kingdom of God" would be. Most people thought the Messiah would be a great ruler like King David, who would overcome all enemies of the Jews and rule over a peaceful kingdom of Israel—or of the whole world. Some people believed that the Messiah would be God's representative, others that he would be God himself. There was also a tradition that the Kingdom of God would be something like a religious assembly, not a political organization like David's kingdom. This was a little closer to Jesus's idea of the Kingdom of God.

What do we know about the mother of Jesus?

Mary was a human being, even though she was the mother of the Son of God. She is venerated in the Christian religion, especially in the Roman Catholic Church, above all other Christian saints.

There are a great many legends about Mary, and their existence is a sign of how important she seemed to the earliest Christians. However, the Bible actually tells us very little about her. Her name only appears once in Mark's Gospel.

Nothing is said about Mary's family, although Elizabeth, mother of John the Baptist, is described as her cousin. Elizabeth came from a family of priests, so perhaps Mary did too. Mary must have been confident in Jesus's powers, because it was she who persuaded him to change water into wine at the wedding in Cana—Jesus's first miracle.

Roman Catholics believe that Mary, unlike all other human beings, was without sin, from birth to death. They also believe that she did not die but, like Jesus, was taken up into Heaven.

What kind of work did Joseph do?

Joseph, the father (or stepfather) of Jesus, was a carpenter by trade. Everyone knows this, though the Bible does not say it in so many words. Matthew says (Chapter 13, verse 55) that, when people were surprised by Jesus's preaching, they asked, "Is not this the carpenter's son?" According to Mark, what the people said was, "Is not this the carpenter?" So we can be fairly certain that Joseph was a carpenter and that Jesus, who did not begin his ministry until he was nearly 30 years old, followed the same trade.

Why did Mary and Joseph travel to Bethlehem? Matthew 2, Luke 2

When Jesus was born, Palestine was under Roman rule. Every few years, the Romans carried out a census, when all the population was counted. The aim was to get a record of tax payers. Although it was very inconvenient for many people, everyone had to register in the town of his birth. No one was excused.

Joseph came from Bethelehem, the city of David, according to the accounts in Matthew's and Luke's Gospels. He therefore had to travel from Nazareth to Bethlehem, with his wife Mary, although she was expecting a baby very soon.

Where was Jesus born? Matthew 2, Luke 2

As everyone knows, Jesus was born in the stable of an inn in the city of Bethlehem. The inn itself was full—probably because there were a lot of visitors there for the same reason as Joseph. This is the well-known account given by both Matthew and Luke.

It was important to Jewish Christians like Matthew that Jesus, as a descendant of King David, was born in David's city and some scholars say that the Bethlehem story may be only a legend and that Jesus was more likely to have been born in Nazareth. Mark's Gospel seems to suggest that he was, although Mark does not tell the Nativity story. Historians have not been able to discover for certain if there was a Roman census of the Jews at about the time Jesus was born, although the governor of Syria held one in 6 BC (the likely date of Jesus's birth). Of course, it does not really matter where Jesus was born, and there seems to be no good reason not to believe the attractive story of the stable in Bethlehem.

According to tradition, Jesus was born in a stable, and the first outsiders to see him were shepherds.

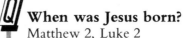

Q When was Jesus born?
Matthew 2, Luke 2

A We celebrate the birth of Jesus on Christmas Day, 25 December. Of course, we do not really know on what day he was born. In fact, we do not know the correct year. Our calendar is supposed to be dated from the year of Jesus's birth, and therefore he ought to have been born at the beginning of the year AD 1 (AD is short for *Anno Domini*, "in the year of the Lord"). But the division between BC ("before Christ") and AD was first made about 500 years later.

The job of working out the year of Jesus's birth was given to a monk in Rome, and he made a mistake in his calculations. We know that King Herod was alive when Jesus was born, and we also know that Herod died in the year 4 BC. Jesus must have been born before that, and Matthew seems to have thought he was born about two years before Herod's death. Therefore, it is now thought that the most likely date is 6 BC.

Who were the first visitors to the baby Jesus? Luke 2

At the time of Jesus's birth, an angel appeared in the fields outside the city walls where some shepherds were looking after the sheep (flocks in the open had to be guarded night and day). They were astonished and frightened, but the angel told them not to be afraid. A joyful event had occurred. A Savior had been born, and they would find him wrapped in swaddling clothes and lying in a manger.

The shepherds rushed off (probably leaving someone behind to watch the sheep), and were amazed to find things exactly as the angel had said.

The story of the birth of Jesus is told in two Gospels, Matthew and Luke, but only Luke mentions the shepherds. It seems right that these simple shepherds should be first to hear the good news and see the infant Jesus—who was to be known later as the "Good Shepherd."

What are swaddling clothes?

Mary wrapped her newborn baby in swaddling clothes, and laid him in a manger—the animals' food box, just the right size for a cradle and filled with soft, warm hay. Some Arab babies are still wrapped in swaddling clothes. They are first wrapped snugly in a cloth and then swaddling bands are wound around, making a tight little bundle. The idea was to save the infant from possible damage, though in fact the bones of young babies are much tougher than people thought. Although the baby was hardly able to move, he was often released from the swaddling clothes, rubbed with oil and dusted with powder. A baby wrapped in this way could be more easily carried on his mother's back while she worked in the fields.

What is the Hebrew word for "family"?

Family life was (and still is) extremely important to the Jews. Almost no one stayed a bachelor or a spinster if he or she could possibly find a wife or husband. Marriages were usually arranged by the parents, as they still are in many Asian countries, although we hear of a few in the Bible in which love played a big part in bringing the couple together.

It was important to have children, especially sons, and the average family in New Testament times probably comprised four or five children at least. The father was very much the head of the household; he had great authority over everyone, adults as well as children.

Family life was well established among the Jews and Jesus strengthened it. The Gospels are full of remarks showing that Jesus admired and respected family life. He remained in his own family, probably working as a carpenter, after he was grown up, and he showed respect as well as love for his mother. (Joseph seems to have died when Jesus was still young).

In spite of the importance of family life, there was no word meaning "family" in Hebrew. The word that is usually translated as "family" in the Bible really means "household."

Who were the Three Wise Men? Matthew 2

After the shepherds came, Wise Men, or Magi, arrived from the East to see the infant Jesus—according to the Nativity story in Matthew's Gospel. These visitors have always been a mystery. They were not "kings" as some legends say, but who and what exactly were they? One modern translation of the Bible calls them astrologers, and obviously they had a good knowledge of the stars. They had noticed a new star and guessed that it meant an important event was about to take place. They had even decided what this event must be, because when they arrived at Herod's court, they asked, "Where is the child who is born to be King of the Jews?"

What guided the Wise Men to the stable? Matthew 2

The Wise Men reached the stable by following a moving star. Some people believe that this was a miracle, others that the star is just a

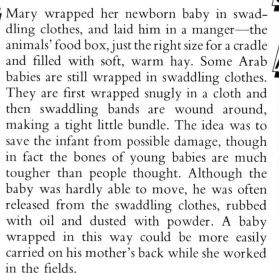

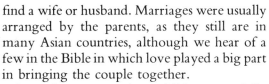

beautiful symbol—not meant to be taken literally. However, it could well have been some unusual astronomical event. It might have been a meteor, or shooting star; it might have been a nova—when a star suddenly becomes much brighter for a time. It could not, however, have been Halley's comet, which would have been visible in 11 BC—unfortunately, too early to fit in with the birth of Jesus. Although astronomers today can tell what was happening in the sky thousands of years ago, the difficulty with the star of the Nativity is that we do not know for certain when Jesus was born.

What are frankincense and myrrh?

The Wise Men came to the baby Jesus to pay homage to him, since they had deduced that he would become a great king. Therefore they brought him precious gifts—gold, frankincense and myrrh.

Frankincense is a pleasant-smelling substance which comes from a certain kind of tree. It appears on the bark as a drop of whitish gum, perhaps as large as a fingernail. The Jews used it in worship—burning it to make a sweet-smelling smoke—and it was also one of the ingredients in the holy oil used in the ceremony of anointing. It was not found in Palestine but was imported from Arabia.

Myrrh is rather similar, coming from another Arabian tree or shrub in the form of yellowish gum. It, too, was used in holy oil, and also as a mild painkiller.

How was incense burned?

Burning incense to make a sweet-smelling smoke was part of Jewish religious ceremony—and later became part of Christian ceremony. The smoke was thought to conceal the presence of God.

Incense was a mixture of several substances, including frankincense and various powdered herbs. It had to burn slowly and steadily, and give off the right amount of smoke. Nearly 1 kilogram (2 lb) of it was used in the Temple daily. There was a special small altar in the Holy Place where it was burned by the high priest every morning. When a priest entered the Holy of Holies, he carried burning incense in a container known as a censer.

The Magi, or "Wise Men," are mysterious figures. They are mentioned only in Matthew's Gospel.

Why did Herod wish to find Jesus? Matthew 2

The Wise Men from the East told King Herod they had come to see the child who would be king of the Jews. Now, Herod was himself king of the Jews at that time, and although he was an old man (he died within about two years of the birth of Jesus), he was alarmed when he heard of a child who would be a threat to his throne. He did not mean to deprive his sons of their share of the kingdom he ruled over. He asked the Wise Men to return to him when they had found the child and tell him where Jesus was, in order that he, too, could go and pay homage. His real intention was, of course, to see that Jesus was killed, because he was a possible threat to the kingdom.

Was King Herod a Jew?

Herod's family came from Edom, or Idumea (its Greek name), the region south of Judea. His grandfather had been converted to Judaism, and Herod was a Jew in terms of his religion. He showed his respect for that religion by rebuilding the Temple on a grand scale. However, he was not Jewish by race, and his subjects in Judea always regarded him as a foreigner. Although he had become king of Judea, with the support of the Romans, in 40 BC, Herod was forced to besiege Jerusalem and did not gain entry to the capital city until three years later.

How did the Wise Men avoid Herod? Matthew 2

Matthew's Gospel says that the Wise Men were warned in a dream not to go back to Herod, and therefore returned home by another road. If they were warned in a dream while sleeping, then they must have spent the night in Bethlehem. It would be interesting to know where they slept!

Obviously, the Wise Men knew their way around, if they could so easily take another road. This has led some people to believe they were merchants or traders, the sort of men who would know all the main international roads.

Why did Joseph decide to go to Egypt? Matthew 2

After the Wise Men had left, Joseph had a dream in which an angel appeared and warned him to take Mary and the baby Jesus to Egypt at once, as Herod was searching for the child to kill him.

When Herod could not find the child, he flew into a rage and ordered that all children under the age of two who had been born at this time of year (that is, when the star appeared) should be killed. This may have been quite a small number, though it is still a horrible deed. Herod, especially in his old age, was very cruel and given to rages. He had already murdered children of his own.

Matthew liked the idea of Jesus going to Egypt, because it had an echo of history. Moses had come out of Egypt, and Matthew thought of Jesus as a Moses-like figure.

For whom did Luke write his Gospel?

We do not know very much about the writers of the Gospels, and the little we do know, or think we know, cannot be proved.

Nearly all the writers of the Bible—Old Testament and New—were, naturally, Jewish. But Luke is thought to have been a Gentile, and to have written his Gospel especially for non-Jewish Christians in the early years of Christianity. Tradition says that he also went with St Paul on his travels, and that he was a physician by profession. The knowledge of medicine he shows in his Gospel seems to prove this.

Luke's Gospel was written later than Mark's, and some parts of Luke are based on Mark. Other parts are very like Matthew and probably came from the same source. Luke said he had never seen Jesus himself, but had talked to those who had.

Who lived in Galilee?

Jesus grew up in Nazareth, a small, otherwise nondescript town in Galilee, the northernmost part of Palestine. Although Galilee was very fine farming country, producing rich grain

122

harvests, and with good pasture and orchards, it had a troubled history because of its position across the main route of conquering armies. It contained a mixed population, including many foreigners and not many "pure" Jews. The Jews of Jerusalem looked down on Galileans in the way that city people often looked down on people from the country, but also because Galileans had this mixed racial background.

As well as Jesus himself, nearly all his disciples came from Galilee. Among the Twelve there was only one who came from Judea—and that was Judas Iscariot!

What furniture did houses contain?

The houses of ordinary people in ancient Palestine contained very little furniture. There was a woolen curtain, woven in the home, which divided the women's sleeping place from the men's. The beds they slept on were generally mats, which could be rolled up out of the way during the daytime. There might be a low table, like a tray on four short legs, and a few low stools. That was all, except for small things like a candlestick, a baby's cradle made of wood, lamps, bowls, pots and pans.

Of course, the house of a rich man, or the palace of a governor, contained grander things, and there would be more chests and boxes for storage. The Romans were fond of couches; they even ate their meals lying on them. Rich people slept on beds which, though they did not have springs, had bands of material stretched across on which they could lie comfortably.

What was a Nazarene?

Matthew's Gospel says that Joseph and his family, when they returned from Egypt, settled down in Nazareth. With his usual desire to link the story of Jesus to the words of the Prophets of the Old Testament, Matthew says that this fulfilled the ancient prophecy that the Messiah should be a Nazarene (a man from Nazareth). However, this is a puzzle, because nowhere in the Old Testament can this prophecy be found!

Jesus was indeed called a Nazarene in later years, and the earliest Christians in Palestine were known as Nazarenes too.

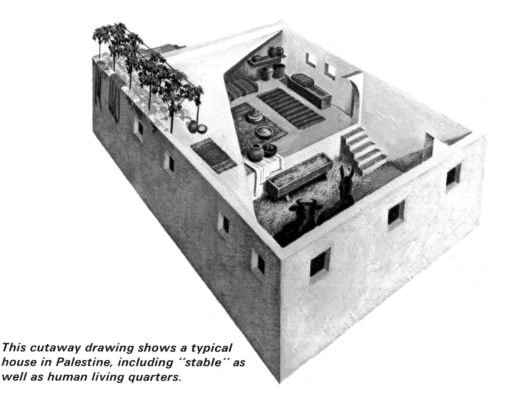

This cutaway drawing shows a typical house in Palestine, including "stable" as well as human living quarters.

How did the boy Jesus get lost?
Luke 2

When Jesus was 12 years old, he went to Jerusalem with his parents for the Feast of the Passover—something that religious Jews tried to do every year. The city must have been terribly crowded, and perhaps it is not so surprising that Joseph and Mary started home without their son, thinking that he was somewhere among the large band of people with whom they were traveling. When they discovered their mistake, they turned back to Jerusalem. After a long search, they found him at the Temple, listening to the learned men discussing the Law, and having plenty to say himself, so that everyone was amazed at his knowledge and intelligence.

It may seem strange, first, that parents could lose sight of a 12-year-old child all day without getting worried, and that a boy of that age should be found discussing learned matters with his elders. But in those days, a boy in Palestine grew up very fast. At this age, Jesus's education would be nearly finished and he would soon be taking up his father, Joseph's trade.

What happened on the roofs of houses?

The houses of ordinary people in Palestine were not really very comfortable, being rather stuffy, dark and smoky. People therefore spent a lot of their time on the flat roof of the house. Visitors might be entertained there, and the family might even sleep there on very hot nights. The roof, like the floor inside, was surfaced with mud. After it rained, the roof would be rolled, like a lawn, with a stone roller.

What happened in the Temple in Jesus's day?

The Temple that Jesus knew was the third Temple of Jerusalem, which was begun by Herod the Great about 15 years before Jesus was born but not completely finished until many years later.

It was much larger than Solomon's Temple but the central building was much the same as before. The Holy of Holies now contained nothing—the precious Ark of the Covenant disappeared when Solomon's Temple was destroyed. It was surrounded by a great number of other buildings: palaces, courtrooms, porches, domes and towers, butcheries, prison cells, barracks, altars, a treasury, a library, and many more. Several thousand priests worked there, and the whole area, which was about the size of 30 tennis courts, was busy and noisy. Only priests were allowed inside the Holy Place and the Holy of Holies, but everywhere else was full of people.

Writing tools: (a) pen and ink holder; (b) ink pots; (c) writing tablet; (d) papyrus sheets; (e) metal pen

Who were the Scribes?

Early civilizations in Mesopotamia and Egypt employed scribes as clerks, keepers of records (which they made on clay tablets), secretaries and so on. In Palestine, they were especially connected with the Temple and the priests.

Scribes in the New Testament were not priests, although they worked closely with them. They sat in the Sanhedrin, the supreme court of Judea. They made copies of the Scriptures—the word "scribe" means "writer"—and they also interpreted them and taught them. They were not paid, so they had to be fairly rich men or else able to make a living outside their duties as scribes. They were often associated with the Pharisees, and they were, like the Pharisees, usually against the teachings of Jesus, because Jesus was not a slave to the old traditions and did not give the scribes the respect they thought they deserved.

Q What do we know about Jesus's childhood?

A Nothing about Jesus himself is really important until he began his mission, when he was almost 30 years old. All the same, most of us would love to have some account of his life as a child. Of the four Gospels, neither Mark nor John say anything at all about Jesus personally until he began to preach. The other two Gospels tell us about his birth, but except for Luke's story about Jesus becoming lost and being found in the Temple-when he was 12, they tell us nothing more until he became linked with John the Baptist, not long before he began his own mission.

Q What kind of education did Jesus have?

A We do not know anything about the education of Jesus, but we can presume he had the same sort of education as other boys of his time. Girls were mostly educated at home.

The Pharisees had been responsible for setting up schools in the synagogues all over Palestine, which boys attended from the age of six. They learned to read and write in Hebrew, which was not their everyday language (they spoke Aramaic). Most subjects were connected with Scripture and the Law, and there was a lot of learning by heart. Pupils had wooden tablets coated with wax, on which they wrote out parts of the Scriptures. Teachers were held in

Schools in Palestine in New Testament times were less formal than ours. However, boys received a thorough religious education, and the Bible gives much evidence of a good knowledge of the Law and the Prophets among ordinary people.

respect, and were paid by the local people.

There were also more advanced schools in the synagogues for those boys of about 15 and over who would themselves become teachers, or rabbis. We do not know positively whether or not Jesus attended one of these, but it is almost certain that he did because of his great knowledge of the Scriptures.

The people seem to have been eager for religious teaching, and this was one reason why Jesus attracted such big crowds when he became a teacher himself.

125

How did boys learn a trade?

 School did not last all day, and boys also had to learn a trade. Most trades in ancient times were hereditary—the children learned their trade from their parents. The son of a carpenter was therefore likely to become a carpenter himself. Girls learned all the domestic jobs from their mothers. Life was not easy, and most people had to work hard, starting from about the age of 13.

 ## When did John the Baptist begin his mission? Luke 1

John the Baptist, who was probably about six months older than his cousin Jesus, came from priestly families on both his father's and his mother's side. He was therefore a priest by birth, the priesthood being hereditary. However, some time in his 20s, he chose to live a hard and lonely life away from civilization, which allowed him to think more clearly. Eventually, he became a preacher. He must have been nearly 30 by that time and we do not know how long he lived his hermit's life before he began to preach his message.

He appeared very like one of the Old Testament prophets—his preaching was equally fiery—and he was often compared with Elijah. From the first, he saw himself as the forerunner of someone greater, for whom he was preparing the way.

 ## What are locusts?

Locusts are insects like grasshoppers, which form enormous swarms and move across the countryside, eating everything green. They can sometimes strip the land bare over thousands of miles, though fortunately these plagues of locusts (one of which was among the plagues of Egypt in the days of Moses) do not happen very often. Locusts are edible, although not everyone would like to eat them.

The English word "locust," in the Bible, is used for several different words in the original Hebrew. Not all the Biblical "locusts" were therefore the same insect, but they were all grasshoppers of a sort.

 ## Could anyone live on locusts and wild honey?

When John the Baptist lived in the wilderness, he wore a rough coat of camel's hair and ate, so the Bible says, "locusts and wild honey." It would be possible to live, for a time anyway, on such a diet, but this is a poetical way of saying that John the Baptist lived a hard existence and ate only what he could find in the wild, as the earliest human beings did. There were other things—plants, berries and so on—growing in the wilderness which he could eat.

 ## What kinds of animals lived in the desert?

The wilderness of Judea was not all desert, as we think of it. It was wild country that was too dry for human settlement, but it was the home of many animals, three of which are pictured here. The vulture, a bird of prey which eats mostly dead creatures, was treated with some respect in Palestine, although it was classed as "unclean" (which means that John the Baptist would not have eaten vulture's eggs).

Another animal he might have seen was the caracal, a type of lynx or bobcat about the size of a fox. Perhaps he also saw vipers, a name he applied to the Pharisees and Sadducees, whom he condemned for their false pride.

Who were the Pharisees?

The Pharisees were a Jewish sect, or group, that began in the 2nd century BC. Their name means "separated," because they separated themselves from the people—although they did so less than either of the other two sects, the Sadducees and the Essenes. The Pharisees insisted on strict obedience to the law of Moses, but they also added new rules and regulations.

They were narrow-minded toward other people. They hated the Romans—and all foreigners—and this made them popular with ordinary people. They were also, on the whole, opponents of Jesus, and partly responsible for the Crucifixion.

Jesus had no time for them, because they had become so absorbed in arguing about minute

Vultures (above), vipers (top right) and lynxes (bottom right) were among the animals that shared the "wilderness" with John the Baptist.

details of the Law that they had no room in their hearts for human sympathy and understanding. He attacked them ferociously, and therefore we get a worse idea of the Pharisees than they deserve. During the 200 years or so when they were most influential, they were largely responsible for preserving the existence of Judaism. They found (and controlled) the synagogues and played a big part in religious education.

Q **What is the meaning of baptism?**

A Baptism became the most important rite in the Christian Church, and is traced back to John the Baptist, the forerunner of Jesus. He called upon the people to repent, and if they did so, they were symbolically washed clean of their sins by being dipped in the River Jordan. (Baptism then meant the whole body had to be wetted, which is still the method used by some Christian churches today.)

John the Baptist did not invent the ceremony of baptism. Such a ceremony had been used for Gentiles who adopted Judaism, and similar rites existed in other religions.

Jesus accepted baptism from John the Baptist, but he never baptized anyone himself, nor did he instruct his disciples to baptize Christian converts. But the ceremony was used by them from the beginning of the Christian Church.

Q **How did John the Baptist influence Jesus?** Mark 1

A All the Gospels record how Jesus was baptized, along with crowds of others, in the River Jordan by John the Baptist. John had said that he was not a new Elijah, nor any other Prophet, nor was he the Messiah. He was the forerunner of someone whose sandals, he said, he was not fit to touch. He seems to have recognized Jesus as that someone, for he tried to persuade him not to be baptized. Instead, he said, Jesus ought to baptize *him*. However, he agreed to do as Jesus asked.

After his baptism, Jesus saw a vision, and a voice from heaven was heard, saying, "This is my beloved Son." This was the moment when Jesus recognized his mission. He already knew that some special task lay ahead of him, but it was now, after the baptism, that he recognized what that task was.

Some taxes were paid in goods, some in cash. Tax collectors had to hand over a fixed amount but they were not prevented from collecting more when they could, and keeping the difference.

Why were tax collectors so unpopular?

In the New Testament, tax collectors are spoken of as if they were one of the most undesirable groups in society. Of course, for some people income tax collectors are not very popular today, but we do not think of them in the same way as we think of drug dealers or muggers.

The job of the tax collectors was to collect the taxes on salt, certain foods and land on behalf of the Roman government (for, by this time, Palestine was under direct Roman rule). However, they squeezed as much tax from people as they could, more than the amount due, and kept the rest for themselves.

How did the Holy Spirit appear after Jesus's baptism?

Matthew's Gospel describes this event in these words: "The heavens were opened unto him, and he saw the Spirit of God descending like a dove, and lighting upon him." The other three Gospels use much the same words, but in John, they are spoken by John the Baptist as a witness of the event.

Doves and pigeons belong to the same family, and when the Bible says "dove," it may equally well mean "pigeon." Of course, pigeons were used as messengers from the earliest times: they were one of the first animals to be put to work by people. On the other hand, the dove was a symbol of peace—of quarrels ended. For these reasons, a dove or pigeon was a very suitable symbol of the Holy Spirit—the Spirit of God descending to earth from heaven.

What did Jesus mean by the Kingdom of God?

Many people came to believe that Jesus was the Messiah, the Deliverer or Savior promised centuries ago by Micah and other Prophets. The purpose of the Messiah, the Prophets said, was to establish the Kingdom of God, or the Kingdom of Heaven. (To the Jews, this was the same thing—they did not like using the name of God directly and often found ways like this to avoid it.)

Jesus came to earth to establish the Kingdom of God, but his kingdom was of a very different sort than the kingdom that most people expected. It had nothing to do with conquests and battles over enemies, or with politics and power. It did have something to do with human happiness, but a type of happiness that could not be gained in the way that many people supposed. Jesus's Kingdom of God was a state of mind, or a state of the soul. It meant accepting the misfortunes of life, such as being poor or ugly, without useless regrets, trying always to do the right thing, loving other people and (therefore) loving God.

Who was St Matthew?

Matthew was the name of one of the Twelve Disciples of Jesus. He was possibly the same man as the tax collector called by Jesus, whose name was Levi. Otherwise, we know nothing about him.

This St Matthew was not the author of the Gospel named after him, although it is possible that some of Matthew's Gospel is based on stories related by the disciple named Matthew. Otherwise, Matthew's Gospel closely follows that of Mark (though it contains many things which are not in Mark), and all Bible scholars now agree that Mark's Gospel was written first. But Mark's Gospel could not have been written much earlier than AD 75. That would mean that Matthew would have been a very, very old man if he had written the Gospel himself, and there are other reasons why he could hardly have done so. For example, the Gospel was written in Greek, and it is unlikely that any of the Twelve Disciples, who were simple men, would have known Greek.

Why did Jesus go off into the wilderness?

The desert approaches the edge of the Jordan valley, and after being baptized by John the Baptist and experiencing the vision in which the Holy Spirit descended on him, Jesus was able to move away quickly into a wild, uninhabited country. He naturally wanted to be as far as possible from the noisy crowds around John the Baptist—to be by himself, to think about the task that lay before him.

Many other people have found that, when they want to think seriously about their lives, it is easier to do it somewhere away from other human beings.

How was Jesus tempted by the Devil?

The Devil came to test Jesus's resolve when he was weak with hunger. The first test, when the Devil invited him to turn stones into bread, was all the more powerful because Jesus *was* hungry. The Devil was also testing Jesus by inviting him to take the easy way out by relying on miracles.

These temptations, or tests, of Jesus probably went on only in his mind. It would have been possible for the Devil to take him to a high mountain, from which he could see a very long way (though not quite "all the kingdoms of the world"), but since the Devil also took him to the parapet of the Temple of Jerusalem, it seems more likely that all the temptations were actually Jesus's own thoughts. That would not have made the tests any easier.

What was Jesus's first miracle? John 2

What seems to have been the first miracle associated with Jesus was filling up the wine jars at the wedding in Cana when the supply of wine was in danger of running out. Jesus performed the miracle at the request of his mother, the one person who had always known who he really was. As Jesus had arrived at the wedding with at least five disciples, he may have been responsible for the wine running out.

It is a simple story, but like all Gospel stories about Jesus, especially those told by John, there is a deeper meaning—and perhaps more than one. For example, did John want us to think of the old wine, which was running out, as the old religion of Judaism, and the new wine as Christianity?

The town of Cana, where Jesus performed his first miracle, has disappeared, but it was probably at Khirbet Qana, about 9 miles (14 km) from Nazareth, where ruins from Roman times have been found.

Why was John the Baptist imprisoned?

Herod Antipas was a son of King Herod the Great, but he ruled only the small province of Galilee. He had run off with his half-brother's wife, a princess named Herodias, and divorced his own wife to marry her. This was, of course, against the Law, and John the Baptist had denounced Herod's action. Herod would have had him killed, because he also was afraid he might lead a revolt. But when he talked to him, he fell under the Baptist's spell, recognizing that he was a true man of God. However, John the Baptist was held in prison for about a year.

What message did John the Baptist send to Jesus?

John the Baptist had always said that he was not the Messiah, but his job was to prepare the way for him. When Jesus came to him to be baptized, John seemed to recognize that this was the man for whom he was preparing the way. According to John's Gospel, the Baptist actually saw the Holy Spirit descend upon Jesus from heaven.

However, after he had been in prison for about a year, he sent two friends to Jesus, asking him if he really was the Messiah, or if there was someone else to come.

Jesus had not claimed to be the Messiah, and although he had performed miracles, his activities did not seem to be what the Baptist and others expected. Nor did Jesus give a direct answer to this question. He told the Baptist's messengers to tell him what they had seen—the lame walking, the blind seeing, the Gospel ("good news") preached to the poor.

Who was Salome?

Salome was the daughter of Herodias and the stepdaughter of Herod Antipas, governor of Galilee. She was a beautiful young woman, and it seems that Herod was very fond of her. Although she only appears in one episode in the New Testament, her story has been told in plays and books. Operas have been written about her.

One rather strange thing about Salome is that she is not mentioned by that name in the New Testament. However, she is mentioned by the Roman-Jewish historian, Josephus, who was born in Jerusalem soon after the Crucifixion, and it is only through Josephus that we know her name.

What did Herod promise his stepdaughter?

The birthday of Herod Antipas was celebrated with a grand party, at which Salome performed a dance. Herod was so pleased with her dancing that, in front of all the guests, he promised to give her anything she asked for. Salome requested that she might first consult her mother.

Herodias, Salome's mother, now had her chance. She hated John the Baptist and had already tried to persuade her husband to have him killed. Herod, who admired the Baptist, had refused, but kept him in prison. Herodias now persuaded her daughter to ask for the head of John the Baptist on a dish.

Herod was unhappy, but he felt he could not break his word in front of all his guests. He therefore commanded his guards to go to the prison and cut off John the Baptist's head. The dreadful head was brought in on a plate, as Salome had asked, and presented to her. She passed it to her mother.

Did trees grow in Palestine?

Much of Palestine is desert, or near-desert, and trees were rather scarce, even in Biblical times. There were even fewer in watery Babylon. When large supplies of timber were needed— for instance, to build the Temple—they had to be imported.

Of course, there were many trees that *did* grow in Palestine. Those mentioned most often in the Bible are olive trees and fig trees. Almonds, pomegranates and date palms are also named. In Biblical times, there were forests of several kinds of oak in the mountains of Judea. The groves of evergreen oaks were probably the ones condemned in the Old Testament because pagan religious ceremonies were held there. Another type of oak, the tabor, was common on the Plain of Sharon.

What is an Apostle?

The Greek word from which we get our word "apostle" means "ambassador," or an important representative of some greater person or power. The Twelve Disciples of Jesus, his first and most important followers, came to be called apostles because they were the representatives of Jesus to the rest of the world. They had known him as nobody else had, and they were his witnesses, who proclaimed his message to the earliest Christians.

What kind of men were Jesus's disciples?

The disciples of Jesus were mostly ordinary working men of Galilee, with no special education. They are sometimes said to have been simple or even primitive men—and certainly they often had difficulty in following Jesus's meaning—but they were not as simple as their opponents liked to claim. To sophisticated city people like the Sadducees and Pharisees in Jerusalem, they appeared to be a group of rough northerners (in those days of poor transport, Galilee was a long way from Jerusalem), but they were not uneducated, and some may have known three languages—some Hebrew and Greek as well as the everyday language of Aramaic. None of them, however, was as well educated as the Apostle Paul, who was not among Jesus's disciples during his lifetime.

Why was Simon renamed Peter?

St Peter, the leading disciple of Jesus and one of his three favorites, is called by several names in the New Testament. He is sometimes called Simon, once Simeon, and several times Cephas, though most often he is called Peter. Simon was his original name. Simeon is a Hebrew version of Simon, and Cephas, which was St Paul's name for him, is an Aramaic version of Peter.

Jesus renamed him Peter because he recognized in this simple fisherman a strong leader or, as he said, "a rock on which I shall build my Church." "Peter," from the Greek *petros*, means "rock." Whenever Peter showed some sign of weakness, Jesus went back to calling him Simon.

Who were called "fishers of men"?

Jesus's first disciple seems to have been Andrew, who had been a follower of John the Baptist. Andrew's brother was Simon, renamed Peter by Jesus, who became the leader of the Twelve Disciples.

When, after John the Baptist had been arrested by Herod, Jesus began preaching, he came across James and John, the sons of Zebedee, as well as Peter and Andrew by the Sea of Galilee. All four men were fishermen by profession. Jesus said "Follow me, and I shall make you fishers of men," meaning that they would become his disciples.

Who were the Twelve Disciples?

The Twelve Disciples of Jesus were young men of about his own age. Jesus had three special favorites—Peter, James, and John—who were always closest to him. This may have been because they understood him best.

We know a lot about the leading disciples as people—St Peter especially. But some of the others among the Twelve are just names. Even Andrew, Peter's brother, is a shadowy figure, and we know nothing of his later life. John's Gospel gives us a few facts about Philip, but does not mention Bartholomew, who may have been the same as the man John's Gospel names as Nathanael.

There are stories about Thomas, Matthew the tax collector, and James the Less—not to mention Judas Iscariot—but we know nothing about Thaddaeus nor about the other Simon, except that he was probably a member of the Zealots, a group of Jewish nationalists. We know Thomas best from the incident (John Chapter 20) where he finally believes in Jesus's resurrection and makes the adoring declaration, "My Lord and My God."

Q What is the importance of the number Twelve?

A Lists of the Twelve Disciples of Jesus are given in four different books of the New Testament. There are small differences in the lists, but the number is always twelve. But was Jesus always accompanied by these Twelve? Were they the only ones who followed him throughout his mission? It seems rather unlikely, especially as several of the Twelve never said or did anything that was significant enough to be reported in the New Testament.

The number twelve is, however, very important in Jewish history, because of the Twelve Tribes of Israel. The fathers of the Twelve Tribes had founded Israel, and in Jesus's time, the Twelve Disciples were seen as the founders of the new kingdom he had come to establish.

Olives were an important crop in Palestine, especially valuable for their oil. This was obtained by crushing with a heavy wheel, turned by a shaft, as in this picture.

Q How long does an olive tree live?

A If you were lucky enough to own an olive grove, you would not have to worry about replanting, and you would not have to do a lot of work to maintain the trees. Olive trees grow well in stony soil and give plenty of fruit every year, once they have passed a certain age. And they go on fruiting for a very long time. Some are known to be centuries old, and with their gnarled and twisted gray trunks, they look it.

Q Who were the Zealots?

A The Zealots were a group of people in Jewish society in the time of Jesus. They were not an organized group, like the Pharisees and the Sadducees, but just people who had the same sort of opinion about politics. They were Jewish patriots, or nationalists, who hated the Roman occupation of their country. Not many Jews actually liked this, but the Zealots were extremists.

One of the Twelve Disciples was called Simon the Zealot. The name helped to prevent him being confused with Simon Peter, the leading member of the disciples. We do not know anything about the beliefs of Simon the Zealot or how they affected his behavior. Some scholars believe that Judas Iscariot may also have been a Zealot.

Q Why were there so many sick people in Palestine?

A It is difficult for us to imagine a world in which there was almost no knowledge of scientific medicine. In Old Testament times, there were no doctors. Illness or disease was thought to be caused by evil spirits, or was a punishment from God, and for centuries after the time of Jesus, medicine remained, to some extent, a matter of magic. Although the Greeks made huge strides in medicine and produced the first real doctors, even in the time of Jesus disease was still thought to be caused by supernatural forces rather than germs—which, of course, no one had heard of.

People suffering from mental illnesses or diseases of the nervous system were said to be

Jesus was not the only person who was said to have cured the sick simply by touching them. These healings testify to the faith of the victim.

"possessed" by a devil. They were cured by "casting out" the devil. Jesus went along with this idea—he could hardly do anything else—when he cured someone of epilepsy or any other nervous complaint.

What is a miracle?

A miracle is an event which cannot be explained by ordinary laws of nature. It is a "supernatural" occurrence. Two thousand years ago, people knew almost nothing of the modern world of science—at least, simple people in Palestine knew nothing (learned Greeks knew quite a lot more). Therefore, a great many things seemed miraculous. For example, to someone who does not know about the movements of the sun, moon and earth, it is a "miracle" when the sun disappears in the middle of the day during an eclipse.

Although many Christian Churches do not expect people to believe in the literal truth of Jesus's miracles, there nevertheless are many Christians for whom they are a source of comfort, and help to strengthen their faith.

Perhaps more than anything else, Jesus's miracles show the power of a powerful personality over others, and how mind is stronger than matter. If you believe in something strongly enough, it can become true: in our own time, people have been cured of deadly diseases in this way.

Many of Jesus's miracles can also be explained as ordinary events. Simple people, who were expecting miracles, could easily believe that a natural event which they did not understand had a supernatural cause. But there is no purpose in trying to think up "scientific" explanations for all these happenings.

Who reached Jesus through a roof?

The first three Gospels all tell the story of the paralyzed man whose friends were unable to bring him into the house where Jesus was because of the crowds of people around him. They carried the man, on his mattress, up to the roof (it was a large house, built around a courtyard) and made a hole in it, through which they lowered the mattress in a rope sling. Jesus was standing below on the verandah, talking to the people in the courtyard.

Although the owner of the house may not have been very pleased, the friends of the paralyzed man did not do as much serious damage as we might think. The roof was made of layers of reeds or brushwood and clay, over wooden beams which rested on the tops of the walls. It was quite a simple task to make a hole in the soft material, remove one or two beams, and lower the man down. Replacing the beams and patching up the hole afterward would take only a few minutes.

Why did Jesus perform miracles?

Jesus always spoke about his miracles as if they were not very important. He did not even call them "miracles," just "works," and it is obvious that he did not really like performing them. He wanted people to believe in what he taught: the Kingdom of Heaven would not get very far if everyone was so impressed by the miracles that they forgot his message. He would not give a "sign from heaven" as a guarantee of his teaching.

However, his miracles were also "signs," as John's Gospel calls them, demonstrating his true nature. Also, Jesus came into the world to help humanity. Could he have refused to heal a sick child just because this would result in the wrong kind of publicity?

Who picked wheat on the Sabbath?

One Sabbath morning, Jesus and his disciples, along with a number of others including several Pharisees, were walking through a field of ripening wheat. The disciples were hungry, and as they walked, they plucked a few ears of wheat, rubbed them between their hands to remove the chaff, and ate the grains.

The Pharisees, always on the lookout for the smallest breach of the Law, were quick to criticize. The Law forbade any kind of work on the Sabbath, and they thought that plucking a few ears of wheat and removing the chaff could be classed as work. It was the same thing as harvesting and threshing.

This narrow-minded interpretation of the Law, typical of the Pharisees, made Jesus angry.

What did Jesus teach about the Sabbath?

Jesus certainly did not intend to overthrow the Jewish Law which went back to Moses. Indeed, he was sometimes enraged by people who flouted it. But what he did mean to do was to attack the idea that the one thing that really mattered was obeying the Law to the letter. The narrow, rigid teaching of the Pharisees put petty rules and regulations before justice or humanity.

It was easy for Jesus to demonstrate to the Pharisees that their attack on his disciples for picking ears of wheat on the Sabbath was silly. Had not King David eaten the Holy Bread from the Temple when he was desperate for food? Did not the priests who were on duty on the Sabbath perform work in the Temple? The Sabbath, he said, was made for people, not people for the Sabbath. In other words, it was a day of worship and rest for people to recover from the week's hard work, not a day for worrying about senseless regulations.

Why was some food considered "unclean"?

The rules governing what food should be eaten and in what way went back to the Law of Moses. Some of the rules seem rather strange, as if they had been invented for no obvious reason. For example, there was a rule (Exodus, Chapter 23) which said that a kid (young goat) should not be boiled in its mother's milk. There seems no reason for such a rule until we discover that, in the religion of the Canaanites, there was a ceremony in which young goats were cooked in this way. The need to keep their religion "pure" and to defend it against the customs of other, "heathen" nations was probably the reasoning behind other dietary rules in the Law of Moses.

However, more important, the rules about "clean" and "unclean" meat showed a very remarkable knowledge about what kind of meat was most likely to do harm. The Law forbade eating animals that do not chew the cud, which, in practice, meant pigs. We know today that pork can be dangerous if not well cooked. Obviously, the ancient Israelites already knew that pork can be risky.

Although many people in the Middle East kept pigs, these animals were non-kosher ("unclean") and therefore religious Jews had nothing to do with them, (see also page 155).

What does *kosher* mean?

The Hebrew word *kosher* means "fit," and as it is usually applied to food, it means "fit to eat." Food that is *kosher* must be not only a certain

kind of food but must also have been prepared in a certain way. Animals must be slaughtered by having their throats cut and all the blood drained out, for instance. (This may sound cruel, but in Biblical times, it was the kindest way possible.) Some food, pork and shellfish for example, was forbidden.

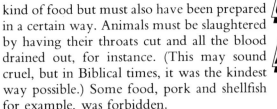

Q What language did Jesus speak?

A The first language of the ancient Hebrews was, of course, Hebrew, which is the language of many Israelis today. However, long before the time of Jesus, the common language throughout the Middle East was Aramaic, which was the official language of the Persian Empire in about 500 BC. Jesus and his disciples probably spoke a local form of Aramaic among themselves, and the four Gospels may also have been first written in that language.

Q In what language was the Bible written?

A In ancient Palestine, a great number of different languages were spoken. Jerusalem must have sounded very like the Tower of Babel!

As we do not have the original versions of all the books of the Bible, we cannot always be certain in what language they were first written. However, most of the Old Testament was written in Hebrew, with some parts probably in Aramaic, and a few words and phrases from most of the dozen or more languages spoken in the neighboring regions. The New Testament was mostly written in a form of Greek which was spoken, usually as a second language, by people with any education in the Middle East in the 1st century AD.

135

Q What is a parable?

A A parable is a story with a special meaning or message which may not be obvious until you think about it. Jesus was, of course, not the only teacher who believed that a lesson will sink in better if it is taught in an interesting way. He wanted people to think about what he said.

When Jesus was asked why he taught in parables, he said that it was to reveal more of the secrets of the Kingdom of Heaven to his disciples. In addition, he wanted to tell a lively story to the crowds who came to hear him, one that might give them something to think about when they were by themselves. They might then come to understand the real point of it, which was always something to do with spiritual life, not the everyday events of the story.

Q Who was the Good Samaritan?
Luke 10

A Jesus probably chose to make a Samaritan the hero of this parable because the Jews of his time looked down on the Samaritans.

Samaria, which lay between Judea and Galilee, had been part of the northern kingdom of Israel during the days of the monarchy. Many of the native people had been driven away by the Assyrians in the 8th century BC, and foreign settlers were moved in, resulting in a mixed population. This later caused a division between the Samaritans and the Jews of Judea. It was made worse after the Jews returned from the Babylonian Captivity, when the Samaritans' offer to help rebuild the Temple was rejected.

Samaritans were not Jews, but they were not quite Gentiles either. Their religion was very close to Judaism, and included a belief in a Messiah. However, they were forbidden to mix with the Jews. Jews were not allowed to marry a Samaritan, and Samaritans were not allowed to worship in Jerusalem. They were an oppressed people, and suffered under the Romans, and Jesus was therefore sympathetic toward them. Later, after the Resurrection, Jesus commanded the disciples to go and preach in Samaria.

Q Who were the Levites?

A Members of the tribe of Levi, one of whom was Aaron, are supposed to have had special duties looking after the Tabernacle in the days of Moses. They were assistant priests—but they were not (unless they were descendants of Aaron) priests themselves.

Jesus was critical of Levites, as he was of most officials, although he did not attack them as a group. He did, however, make one of the travelers who ignored the wounded man in the parable of the Good Samaritan a Levite.

Q What were inns like?

A Two inns are mentioned in the New Testament—the inn at Bethlehem where Jesus was born, and the one where the Good Samaritan took the wounded man.

There was a tradition of hospitality to travelers and other strangers in ancient Palestine. When Jesus sent his disciples off to preach in different parts of the country, he expected the local people to give them food and lodging. As a rule, you were better off staying in a private house than you were in an inn. Inns were simply places where a traveler could find shelter for himself and his animal (or animals). Often, they did not provide food or drink, or even a bed; travelers brought these things with them. Mary and Joseph were really not so badly treated when they had to sleep in the stable—the rest of the guests were probably not much more comfortable.

There was a tradition of hospitality to travelers in ancient Palestine, and people were usually willing to provide a bed or a meal. Inns were probably used mostly by those traveling with a number of animals, requiring shelter and not much more.

Q What did Jesus mean by the word "love"?

A A scribe once asked Jesus which was the greatest of the Ten Commandments. He replied that the first and greatest commandment is to love God, and the second is to love your neighbor. (Scribes liked to argue about things like this. Jesus's answer was very good, because if you obey these two commandments, you are bound to obey all the others.)

"Love," however, meant much more than just a feeling of fondness. It is also said that God *is* Love. To love God is to become one with him. God's love is sometimes translated in the Bible by the word "charity," which has now taken a rather different meaning. Then it meant kindness, caring, good will and tolerance—without limit.

Q What are the Beatitudes? Matthew 5

A It is by loving God, Jesus said, that a person enters the Kingdom of God, but people of a certain sort are more likely to do this than others. Matthew's Gospel gives a list of the kind of people who, Jesus said, are blessed—such as "the meek," "the merciful," "the pure in heart." This list is known as the Beatitudes. The word means "blessed ones" or just "blessings." They are part of the passage sometimes called the Sermon on the Mount.

Q What does the title "rabbi" mean?

A "Rabbi" was the word used most often by the disciples of Jesus when they spoke to him. In the King James Bible, it is translated as "Master." In New Testament times, any learned man might be called "Rabbi."

However, strictly speaking, a rabbi was, first of all, a teacher, a man learned in the Law, but he was also a guide and a father-figure among his people. He was expected to be dignified, kind to all, and to preach every Sabbath in the synagogue. He was not paid, and therefore, unless he happened to be rich, he had to earn his living in the same way as everyone else. It is only in the last 500 years that rabbis have been paid a salary.

Q Who were the Romans?

A When Jesus was alive, Rome was the greatest power in the world, its empire stretching across most of Europe and the Middle East as well as North Africa. Beginning as a small Italian tribe, the Romans had built up a strong democratic republic, but by the time of Jesus's birth, this had given way to what was really a military dictatorship, ruled by an emperor. Because the Roman empire covered such a large area, the government in Rome often allowed the subjects in distant territories to continue life without much interference and under their own rulers, provided they remained loyal to Rome and paid their taxes.

Roman civilization—ideas, art, customs—was based on the earlier civilization of Greece, and educated Romans could speak Greek as well as their own language, Latin.

Q What was a centurion?

A The soldiers on duty in Palestine were not Romans but troops hired and trained in the provinces of the empire. In Palestine, they were mostly Syrians. They were commanded by Roman officers, however. A centurion was a junior officer, roughly the equivalent of a lieutenant or a captain in a modern army. He was so called because, in theory, the number of soldiers in his command was 100—a "century" —but in practice, there were often fewer.

Five centurions are mentioned in the New Testament, and three of them became followers of Jesus, including the centurion who was in charge of the guards at the Crucifixion.

Q What is alabaster?

A The woman who anointed the feet of Jesus when he was eating in the Pharisee's house brought the ointment, which was oil of myrrh, in a small alabaster jar. Alabaster is a stone like marble that is white or creamy in color, and it was used for making jars for precious fluids, as well as other small containers such as lamps, in very ancient times. Such jars have been found in Mesopotamia dating from about 1,000 years before the time of Abraham.

Jesus preaching to the crowds by the Sea of Galilee.

Whom did Jesus raise from the dead? John 11

Several people are said to have been restored to life by Jesus after they had died. The most famous of these was Lazarus, who was the brother of Jesus's friends Mary and Martha. They lived in Bethany, outside Jerusalem, and when Lazarus was taken ill, Jesus was away on the other side of the River Jordan. By the time he arrived, Lazarus had been dead and in his tomb for three or four days.

Unlike other stories such as the reviving of Jairus's daughter (when the girl could have been in a coma rather than actually dead), this one cannot be explained away by those who like to look for ordinary explanations of the miracles. For that reason, and because the resurrection of Lazarus is related only in John's Gospel, some Biblical scholars have wondered whether every detail of the story is true.

What is nard? John 12

When Jesus was staying with Mary and Martha in Bethany during the week before Passover, Mary bought an expensive perfume —oil of nard—to anoint his feet. (Judas Iscariot, who was there, thought it ought to have been sold and the money given to the poor.) "Nard" is short for "spikenard", *Nardostachys jatamansi*, a plant with spiky flowers, from which the sweet-smelling ointment is obtained.

138

Neville Dear

 Why did Jesus preach from a boat?

 When Jesus was teaching on the shore of the Sea of Galilee, a great crowd came to listen to him. Standing on the shore with so many pressing around him, it would have been difficult for people to hear or see him. But by getting into a boat and pushing it out a short way from the shore, he could put a little distance between himself and the crowd. It was almost like standing on a stage—or in a pulpit.

 What was the parable of the sower?
Mark 4

Jesus taught in parables partly because in that way he could use simple everyday incidents, which everyone understood, to teach messages which were not so easy to understand. He told the parable of the sower when he was preaching from a boat in the Sea of Galilee—perhaps while there was actually a man sowing in a field within view.

In ancient times, seed was sown by hand, and of course, a lot was wasted. In Jesus's story, some seed fell on the path, where the birds got it. Some fell on stony ground where the layer of soil was so thin that the plants could not get any water and shriveled in the sun.

Some fell among weeds, where the plants were choked by the thistles. And some fell into good soil, where it sprouted, grew, and produced 60 or 100 times as much grain as had been sown.

The grain would be wheat or barley. Although wheat was more valuable, barley grew better on poor soil.

139

How did Jesus explain the parable of the sower?

Matthew's Gospel says that Jesus spoke to the people in parables because, according to prophecy, that is what the Messiah would do. But there was a simpler reason. By telling a story about everyday, familiar things, Jesus gained the attention of his hearers, and afterward, those who took the trouble to think might arrive at the real meaning of the story.

He explained the parable of the sower to his disciples later. The seed was the Word of God, which Jesus preached. For some people, no sooner did they hear the Word than they heard something else which occupied all their attention (i.e. the seed on the path). Some people took up the message eagerly for a time, but then lost interest (i.e. the seed on stony ground). Some heard and understood, but they were so busy with the cares and woes of everyday life that their faith in God's word died (i.e. the seed fallen among weeds). But some heard and understood the Word of God and made it part of their lives (i.e. the seed fallen on good soil).

Seed was sown by hand—the only method until as recently as the 18th century.

How did farmers store their grain?

A farmer had to pay some of his grain in taxes, and the government had large storehouses where such grain was kept under guard. The rest was sold in the marketplace or kept for use at home. Kernels of grain might be stored in big jars—the kind with two handles and a wide opening at the top. Larger amounts were stored in underground silos. Farmers in Palestine never used barns.

Who was the Son of Man?

In the Old Testament, the Hebrew words which are translated as "Son of Man" are used to describe any man—or rather, any good man. In the New Testament, the "Son of Man" is the name that Jesus often gives himself. It is not used by any of the Gospel writers, however, except when they are quoting Jesus's words directly.

Some people have thought that his use of this name for himself means that Jesus was concentrating on his human, not his godly self. This idea appeals to people who find it difficult to think of Jesus as God. But the fact that the Gospel writers did not use the name was probably not because they feared it denied that Jesus was divine, but because it was a difficult term to understand when translated into Greek.

How often should a sinner be forgiven? Matthew 18

Jesus taught that sinners should be treated with sympathy and understanding—yet another way in which his teaching was different from that of the Pharisees and the other leaders of Judaism in his time.

One day Peter asked him how many times he ought to forgive a man who did him wrong. Would seven times be enough? Jesus's reply was: Not seven times, but seventy times seven —in other words, sinners should be given every possible chance.

What happened to the man who demanded payment of a debt? Matthew 18

After telling Peter that he should forgive someone who had wronged him not seven times but seventy times seven, Jesus told a parable about forgiveness.

A certain king (this story seems to be set in the East, perhaps in Babylon) had an official who owed him a huge amount of money. He was going to force the man to sell all his property in order to pay the debt, but the man begged for time and the king agreed.

Shortly afterward, the same official met another man who owed *him* money, but only a very little. He insisted on being paid at once, and when the man could not pay him, he had him thrown into prison.

When the king heard this, he was furious. The official had refused to show any mercy to someone who owed him very little, although the king had given him extra time to pay his own, huge debt. The king handed him over to the torturers until the debt was paid.

How was grain harvested?

Jesus came from Galilee, which contained some of the most fertile farming land in Palestine, and his parables and teachings are full of talk about farming.

In fact, farming methods in New Testament times had changed very little since the days of King David. The grain was still reaped with an iron sickle: the reaper would catch hold of a bunch of stalks with his left hand and cut through them with the sickle held in his right. The grain would be bound into bundles, or sheaves and probably left to stand in the fields for a few days to dry out. Then the sheaves would be carried by cart to the local threshing floor—there was usually one in each village.

What were the wages of the laborers in the vineyard? Matthew 20

This is another of the parables of Jesus, which he told when he was trying to explain to his disciples what he meant by the Kingdom of Heaven. It is a parable which certainly has a clear message for us today.

The laborers were annoyed because they were paid the same wages as others who had been hired much later in the day and had therefore done less work for the same money. The employer answered them by saying,

"What difference does it make to you? You agreed to work for one day for the usual daily wage. It is none of your business if I choose to pay the same to others whom I hired later."

Jesus was probably thinking again of the Pharisees and the other self-righteous leaders of Judaism. Such people would have said that, after carefully obeying the Law all their lives, they were worth a bigger reward than people who had been sinners and only at the last minute, more or less, were converted by Jesus's preaching. But God, Jesus was saying, is not only just. He is also generous.

What is a vineyard?

A vineyard is a field of vines, which are climbing plants that produce fruit. Different kinds of vines—melons, cucumbers, etc.—are referred to once or twice in the Old Testament, but grape vines are mentioned many times.

Grapes grew very well in Palestine (and still do), and were often grown on terraced hillsides. They were a symbol of luxury to the nomadic Israelites as they approached the Land of Canaan, and to this day, grapes are exported in large amounts by the state of Israel.

Most of the grape crop was used for making wine. However, some were dried to make raisins, and some were eaten fresh.

Jesus often told of the vine and the grape in his parables. At the Last Supper, he used wine to represent his blood that would be shed for the human race.

What did Jesus say about divorce?

The Pharisees, hoping to trip him up, asked Jesus if it were legal for a man to divorce his wife. His reply was: those whom God has joined together, man may not separate. If a wife went off with another man, then her husband might divorce her—but not for any other cause. His disciples said, in that case, it was better not to marry. Jesus agreed that some men are incapable of marriage.

Divorce was very easy at this time. Some rabbis said a man might divorce his wife if he grew tired of her. Jesus taught that marriage was a great deal more important than that.

This type of balance was used in Egypt nearly 3,000 years before Jesus's time.

How were things weighed and measured?

In the Old Testament, weights and measurements are usually rough estimates. For example, a *cubit* was the length of a man's forearm —hardly an exact measurement.

By New Testament times, the old Jewish measures had been adapted to Roman measurements, which were more precise. Thus the cubit was then just under 45 cm (18 in), and the *fathom* (the length of outstretched arms) was 4 cubits (2 m/70 in). The *stade* (mentioned in Luke, Chapter 24) was a Greek measurement equal to about 183 m (600 ft).

The only measurement of weight mentioned in the New Testament is the Roman *pound*, which was slightly less than 340 g (12 oz). When hailstones as heavy as a "talent" are mentioned in Revelation (Chapter 16), the writer is exaggerating—in the same way we might say "This weighs a ton"—because a talent was equal to about 40 kg (90 lb)!

Who kept spare oil for their lamps? Matthew 25

Most people believed that the Day of Judgment would come soon, but they did not know when. Jesus told his disciples that they should be prepared at all times. When he told the story of the girls invited to a wedding, perhaps it was a warning that people might have to wait longer than they supposed.

The ten girls were waiting for the bridegroom to arrive, but he was delayed, and they all dozed off to sleep. At midnight, they were awoken by a shout that the bridegroom was coming. They got up hastily, and found that their lamps were going out. Five of them had no more oil, but the other five were better prepared—they had brought spare oil with them. The first five rushed off to fetch more oil, but while they were away, the bridegroom arrived, and so they missed the wedding feast.

When did Jesus tell the waves to be still? Mark 4

Jesus sometimes liked to get away from the crowds so that he could rest, and think, and pray. One evening after he had spent the whole day by the Sea of Galilee surrounded by masses of people, he said to his disciples, "Let us get into a boat and go over to the other side of the lake."

They did as he suggested, and the exhausted Jesus soon fell asleep in the stern of the boat. Then a sudden fierce storm arose. The waves rushed into the boat and the disciples could not bale fast enough to keep the water out. It looked as though they would sink, and in panic, they woke Jesus, who had been peacefully sleeping through the storm. Jesus was disappointed in them. How small was their trust in God that they should fear drowning while Jesus was with them! He rose to his feet and faced the storm. "Peace!" he said. "Be still!" And the storm died away.

Why is the Sea of Galilee stormy?

The Sea of Galilee, a freshwater lake through which the River Jordan flows, is famous for sudden, violent storms. These are caused by the peculiar form of the land in that area. The lake is low-lying—nearly 215 m (700 ft) below sea level—but partly surrounded by mountains. Storms are caused by sharp changes in air temperature—in this case, between warm air by the lake and cold on the high land behind.

A storm on the Sea of Galilee

The mountains shelter one edge of the lake, but the storm erupts in the middle and whips up the water into high waves on the other side. Jesus was caught in a storm more than once while crossing the lake.

How did Jesus frighten his disciples on the Sea of Galilee? Matthew 14

After a very hectic day on the shores of the Sea of Galilee (it was the day of the miracle of the loaves and fishes), Jesus told his disciples to go home by boat without him while he went up into the hills to pray. On their way, they met a very strong headwind, which actually forced them backward. Jesus had intended to walk along the shore to meet them, but when he saw that they were going to have to land at another place, he (probably) decided to take a short cut across the water, to avoid having to climb another hill.

When the disciples saw him walking on the water, they cried out in terror, thinking they were seeing a ghost. Jesus had to call out to them, "Don't be afraid! It is I!" In spite of all his teaching and earlier miracles, the disciples never really understood just who or what Jesus was.

Why did Peter sink? Matthew 14

When Peter saw Jesus walking on the water, he called out, "Lord, if it is you, tell me to come to you on the water." Jesus said, "Come!" Peter stepped out of the boat and began to walk over the water toward Jesus. But the wind was still very strong, and Peter lost his nerve. "Save me!" he cried, and Jesus reached out a hand to hold him. Together they stepped into the boat, and the wind immediately dropped.

The story of Jesus walking on the water is told by both Matthew and Mark, but only Matthew tells the incident about Peter. It is a good example of Peter's character: he had greater faith than any of the other disciples, but in a crisis, his faith was not quite strong enough.

Who were the Gadarenes?

Gadara, the city and region of the Gadarenes, lay to the southeast of the Sea of Galilee, and was visited by Jesus at least once. The region had been ruled by different people, including for a time the Jews. Gadara was one of a chain of ten cities called the Decapolis, founded in Hellenistic times (some of them, perhaps, by Alexander the Great himself). The Gadarenes were Gentiles (non-Jews), as we can easily tell from the fact that they kept pigs.

Q What happened to the Gadarene swine? Mark 5, Luke 8

A When Jesus met the madman in the land of the Gadarenes, the devils within the man called out, asking not to be cast out because they would then go to hell. If they had to be cast out, they asked that they be allowed to enter into some pigs, which were feeding on a patch of ground nearby. Jesus agreed to this, and those who were there suddenly saw the pigs rush off madly down a slope, and straight into the Sea of Galilee. Every one was drowned.

Q Why was the madman called "Legion"?

A In Luke's gospel, the madman whom Jesus met in the land of the Gadarenes told him that his name was "Legion," "because we are many" —meaning there were many devils inside him. A legion was the largest unit in the Roman army, containing 6,000 men. Perhaps by using the name "Legion" the madman was also suggesting that the devils in him were powerful as well as numerous.

One Biblical scholar has suggested another possible reason for the madman's name. Near Gadara, this researcher had seen the gravestone of a Roman soldier, on which was written that he had belonged to the 14th Legion. Perhaps the madman—who, as the Bible says, lived among the tombs—had seen this word repeated many times and had come to take it as his own name.

Q Why did the Gadarenes ask Jesus to go away?

A When the swineherds, who were in charge of the Gadarene pigs, saw them suddenly go crazy and rush down the hill into the lake, they were terrified and ran to the town, where they told everyone what had happened. People came pouring out of the town to the tombs where the madman lived. There, they found him sitting quietly, perfectly sane. When they heard how the devils that had possessed him had been seen to leave him and enter the pigs, they were just as frightened as the swineherds, and asked Jesus to go away and leave them alone. Jesus, of course, did so. The man who had been called Legion wanted to go with him, but Jesus asked him to stay in his own district and tell people what had happened.

Q How was cloth made?

A Although there were professional weavers working in large workshops in most big towns and cities in Biblical times, cloth—for clothes, curtains, rugs, etc.—was made by the ordinary people of Palestine at home.

It was generally woven on a simple upright loom, of a kind that can still be seen today. The threads of the warp (the vertical threads) hung from a beam and were kept tight by weights at the bottom. Then the (horizontal) threads of the weft were woven in and out of the warp threads with the aid of a little wooden tool called a shuttle.

The most common material for making cloth was sheep's wool, although camel hair, flax (linen), goat's hair and, by New Testament times, cotton, were also used.

Weaving on a horizontal loom, which was kept taut by pegs in the ground.

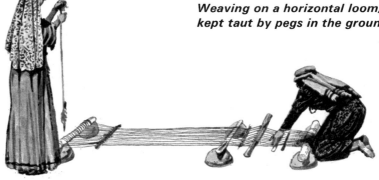

144

Who was Jairus's daughter? Mark 5

We are never told the name of this 12-year-old girl, whom Jesus restored to life and health. Her father, Jairus, is described as one of the presidents of the local synagogue. As such, he would have been in charge of the actual building of the synagogue and of the worship conducted there, and was therefore an important man. As he was only *one* of the presidents, his title may have been an honorary one—the synagogue would have had only one working president. Still, he was obviously a leader of the community, and that such a man should come to Jesus for help shows that he had a great reputation as a worker of miracles.

When the girl had been brought back to life, Jesus told her family to give her something to eat. He realized, if no one else did, that she was weak and needed to build up her strength.

What was Tyrian purple?

Many dyes for coloring cloth were known in Palestine. Most of them came from plants, though the red color for the cloth used in synagogues came from the cochineal insect.

The most expensive dye was purple. It came from the murex, a type of whelk, and a vast number of these mollusks were required for even a small amount of dye—in fact, 9,000 were needed to make 1 g (7/20 oz). Tyre, on the coast of what is now Lebanon, was one of the places where the whelks were gathered, hence the name "Tyrian purple." Because it was worn only by very rich people, especially kings and princes, the color became known as "royal purple."

Why did the sick woman touch Jesus's robe?

While Jesus was going to Jairus's house, followed by a large crowd, a woman who had suffered from an illness for 12 years came up behind him and touched his cloak. No doctor had ever been able to help her, but when she touched Jesus, she was cured at once.

In ancient times, many people believed that certain great healers or medicine men could cure by touch alone. It was thought that some kind of power went out of them into the person who touched them. This belief lasted for a long time. For example, in England as late as the early 18th century, people believed that the king could cure sufferers of the skin disease called scrofula—also known as the "king's evil"—by a touch of his hand.

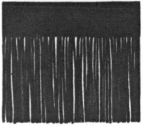

The purple dye so popular in ancient times came from a type of mollusk. It was very expensive, because a huge number of these creatures were needed to make even a small quantity. It is said that about 12,000 were required for a minute portion of dye—enough to color the fringe of a dress.

145

A On his way to Jairus's house, Jesus was jostled to and fro amid the throng. Nevertheless, when the woman forced her way through and managed to reach the tassel on his cloak, he knew that he had been "touched" in a special way. The disciples were amazed—and amused—when he asked, "Who touched me?" because, of course, he was being "touched" by dozens of people every second. We are told that when the woman felt Jesus's eyes on her she was afraid and knelt before him.

This story is told in the first three Gospels. Mark, as always, is careful to explain that the sick woman was not cured simply by magic. He quotes Jesus as saying to her, "Your faith has cured you. Go in peace."

A The main garment worn by men was a loose tunic—made of wool and sometimes colored brightly—with baggy sleeves and reaching to the calves. It was held in at the waist with a cloth belt which also contained pockets. Over the tunic, a cloak was worn—again usually wool—which was not only an overcoat but also a blanket and even, if necessary, a bed. It was rather like the plaid worn by Scottish Highlanders before someone invented the kilt. Devout Jews (including Jesus) had a blue tassel at each corner of the cloak. The sick woman cured by Jesus on the way to the house of Jairus took hold of one of these tassels.

Women and children wore tunics that were very like men's, but these were probably of brighter colors or decorated with embroidery. The clothes of men and women had to be

The type of clothes worn by the Jews in New Testament times was not so very different from the clothes worn in parts of the Middle East today, though then they generally were made of wool rather than cotton. The main garment was a long, loose tunic, longer than that worn by some neighboring peoples. The skirts could be tucked into the girdle for convenience when working.

different, however, for the Law forbade men to wear women's clothes or women to wear men's.

Q Why did Jesus heal the sick?

A The simple answer to this question is that Jesus could not turn away someone who came to him to be cured of an illness, providing that person had faith and really believed that Jesus could and would cure him or her. However, in Biblical times, when medicine as we know it hardly existed, healing the sick was thought to be a divine power—something that God did. This belief existed in other societies too. Both the Babylonians and the Greeks had gods whose special job was healing.

All the same, healing the sick was a problem for Jesus. He was not the only person at that time who was said to have the power of healing, and he did not wish people to believe in him simply because he could work miracles of this kind.

Q What did Jesus say to the leper?
Mark 1

A One day a leper came to Jesus and said, "You could cure me if you wanted to." Mark's Gospel seems to suggest that Jesus was annoyed that the man doubted his willingness to cure him (although what is meant here is not quite clear). In any event, he stretched out his hand and cured the man. Then he said, "Don't say anything to anyone about this, but go and show yourself to the priest."

One of the worst things about being a leper was that you were classed as "unclean" and therefore cast out of the community. Anyone whose leprosy had gone (it seems to have been a different kind of disease from the one we know, which would have been incurable) had to be examined by a priest, who would pronounce him "clean."

The reason Jesus told the man to say nothing about how he had been cured was probably that he did not want to start a fuss. He would have been in trouble with the priests and other authorities, and perhaps he was already worried that the news of his healing powers would distract people from his teaching, the main purpose of his life.

Q Did Jesus preach only to the Jews?
Mark 7

A Jesus was a Jew, born among Jews, who preached to Jews. The Jews had always been very jealous of their religion—keeping out foreigners at all costs. This attitude was not shared by Jesus, even though he naturally considered that his first duty was to the Jews, not the Gentiles. However, a Gentile who showed that he or she had faith did not come to Jesus in vain.

Once when Jesus had gone into a Gentile region for a rest, a woman came to him and begged him to cure her daughter, who was ill at home. Jesus's first answer was that he had been sent to the children of Israel, not to the Gentiles. The Gentile woman would not be put off so easily.

Then Jesus said—probably with a smile— "Is it fair to throw the children's food to the dogs?" The woman made a wonderful answer. "But," she said, "the dogs eat the crumbs that fall from their masters' table." Jesus was impressed by her wit as well as her faith, and told her that her daughter would be well when she got home. This was a rare example of Jesus making a cure without even seeing the sick person.

Q What was the widow's mite?
Mark 12

A There is a saying about giving presents: "It's the thought that counts." The story of the widow's mite goes a lot further than that.

Jesus was teaching in the Temple, near the collecting box. People were dropping money into the box as they passed. Many of them were rich people and they gave large sums of money. Then along came an old woman, a widow, who dropped in two little copper coins (what the King James Bible calls a "mite," meaning very little). Jesus told his disciples that this poor old widow had given more than any of the others, because the others had more than enough to live on, while she had not enough.

147

What was the most important food in the household?

In the Hebrew Bible, the same word is used to mean both "bread" and "food." Bread was the main food in ancient Palestine. The most common sort was made from barley. Wheat bread was nicer, but more expensive. Bread was usually made fresh every day (except on the Sabbath, of course). Sometimes the grain had to be ground by hand; then it was mixed with water to make dough. Yeast was added to make the bread "rise"—except at Passover, when unleavened bread ("leaven" = yeast) had to be eaten. Sometimes, small, round, flattish loaves were baked on a hot stone, with a fire

Grinding grain into flour with a hand mill.

burning underneath. But most houses probably had ovens, shaped something like a bell and made of clay, with a fire at the bottom.

What did Jesus say about healing on the Sabbath? Luke 13

One day when Jesus was teaching in a synagogue, he saw a woman who was deformed. He cured her, and this annoyed the president of the synagogue. People should come to be cured on weekdays, he said, and not on the Sabbath, when no one was supposed to work.

This was the sort of narrow-minded thinking that annoyed Jesus. He had already had trouble with the authorities about the Sabbath (see page 134). Now he said, "Don't you go and give water and food to your animals on the Sabbath? If it is all right to do that, surely it is all right to heal a sick woman?"

Who was the other "Good Samaritan"? Luke 17

When Jesus, on his way to Jerusalem, approached a certain village, there was a group of ten lepers waiting outside. They were not allowed near other people because they were "unclean"—and they were also infectious. When they saw Jesus, they called out to him: "Master, have pity on us!" Jesus called back: "Go and show yourselves to the priests!"

This was another way of saying, "You are cured," because it was the priests' job to certify that lepers were healed and therefore "clean" again.

The men went off and, sure enough, soon found that their skin had cleared up and the disease had miraculously left them. One of them turned back, shouting praises to God, and threw himself at the feet of Jesus in his gratitude. Jesus, shaking his head sadly perhaps, asked him what had happened to the other nine!

The man who had turned back was a Samaritan, and he may have become separated from the others. Another reason could have been that they would have gone to the priests in Jerusalem, but a Samaritan would have gone to the Samaritan temple in Samaria.

What was the pool of Bethesda?
John 5

According to John's Gospel, Jesus went several times to Jerusalem to attend the religious festivals. On one of these visits, he went to the pool of Bethesda, where he cured a man who had been crippled for 38 years. The pool is described as having five colonnades—covered walkways with columns on the open side. This seems an odd number for a pool, which usually had four sides, not five, but it makes sense when we read a description of it by a bishop of Jerusalem who lived in the 4th century. He said that the fifth colonnade ran across the center of the pool, dividing it into two. A pool exactly like this was found by archeologists in Jerusalem 100 years ago.

Crippled people and others suffering from various ailments used to go to the pool because, every now and then, the waters mysteriously "moved." It was thought that this disturbance was caused by an angel, though it may well have been due to a spring from which the water came in occasional spurts (other springs like this are known in Palestine). The first person to enter the water after it had been stirred would be cured. The man Jesus cured complained that he had no one to help him, and therefore someone else always got into the pool before he did.

Very little is known for certain about the writers of Christian scripture. It is clear that much in the Gospels comes from eye-witnesses, but it was probably written down at second hand.

Who wrote the Gospel according to St John?

John's Gospel was probably written near the end of the 1st century AD. It therefore could not have been written by St John the disciple, brother of James and perhaps Jesus's favorite among the Twelve, because he is believed to have died before AD 70. The author also came from Ephesus, which St John did not, and the character of the Gospel writer seems different from what we know of St John.

Many Biblical scholars believe that the Gospel writer was St John the Elder, who came from Ephesus and lived at the appropriate time. However, it is clear that this Gospel, which differs a good deal from the other three, includes first-hand accounts of Jesus, and it seems more than likely that this witness was indeed the disciple, John. The person mentioned several times in this Gospel as "the disciple whom Jesus loved" is probably this John. Perhaps John the disciple dictated it.

However, Bible scholars themselves disagree over all these difficult questions.

Who was Bartimaeus? Mark 10

Bartimaeus was the blind beggar whose sight was restored by Jesus on a road near Jericho. The story is told in detail in the first three Gospels, although only Mark gives the blind man's name. It looks as though the incident was witnessed first-hand—probably by Mark. After his sight was restored, we are told Bartimaeus followed Jesus, praising God.

149

149

How did Jesus feed 5,000 people?
Matthew 14

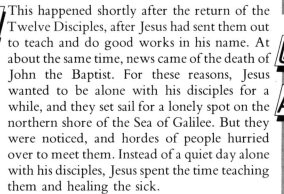

This happened shortly after the return of the Twelve Disciples, after Jesus had sent them out to teach and do good works in his name. At about the same time, news came of the death of John the Baptist. For these reasons, Jesus wanted to be alone with his disciples for a while, and they set sail for a lonely spot on the northern shore of the Sea of Galilee. But they were noticed, and hordes of people hurried over to meet them. Instead of a quiet day alone with his disciples, Jesus spent the time teaching them and healing the sick.

As evening approached, his disciples advised him to send the people home, as they had nothing to eat. Jesus said, "Feed them yourselves." This was a tall order—they had no food nor the money to buy any. They collected as much food as was available, but this turned out to be only five loaves of bread and two fishes. However, this was given out to the people. The supply never ran out, and everyone was fed.

Stories like this are not meant to be pure history. They teach a lesson, like Jesus's parables. Jesus was perhaps testing the faith of his disciples, and also teaching that, "Man does not live by bread alone."

What kinds of fish were eaten in Palestine?

The Bible tells us a lot about food, often in great detail. But it never tells us very much about fish—no fish is mentioned by name, not even the "whale" that swallowed Jonah (it is just "a great fish").

Most of the fish eaten in Palestine came from the Mediterranean, but many freshwater fish from the River Jordan and the Sea of Galilee were also consumed. (There are no fish in the Dead Sea, which is too salty). Fishing was an important business in Galilee, and the first four disciples of Jesus were fishermen.

The two fish which fed the 5,000 probably came from the Sea of Galilee. They could have been bream, dace, barbel, or any of about 12 different species (including one which carries its newly-hatched young in its mouth).

Fish was an important food, but according to Jewish Law, only fish with scales could be eaten. Marine creatures which did not have scales were classed as "unclean."

Who wore sackcloth and ashes?

Sackcloth was a rough kind of cloth that, as its name suggests, might have been used to make sacks. Ashes were what was left after a fire had burned out, perhaps a sacrificial fire in which a body of an animal had been burned. To wear sackcloth and spread ashes on your head was a sign of sorrow, repentance—or protest. This custom is mentioned several times in the Old Testament (for example, David wore sackcloth when mourning over the death of Abner). Jesus also referred to this custom in Luke's Gospel, Chapter 10, verse 13.

Who did people think Jesus was?
Matthew 16

This was a question which Jesus himself asked of his disciples. He was not interested in hearing what other people were saying about him, but he wanted to know what his disciples thought. They answered that some people thought he was John the Baptist or one of the Prophets reborn—Elijah was a favorite because he had never "died" and was expected to return. Jesus then asked, "Who do *you* say that I am?" and Peter made his famous reply, earning himself his place as the first true Christian: "You are the Messiah, the Son of the living God."

This was a very tense time in Palestine. Nearly everyone expected the Messiah to come soon. John the Baptist had appeared like one of the Old Testament Prophets, and other leaders had arisen with powerful political or religious teachings to keep the people in a fever of expectation.

Who did Gospel writers mean by "the Jews"?

The ancient Hebrew people became known as Jews about the time of the Babylonian Exile. In the New Testament, "the Jews" are sometimes

Neville Dear

Mourners at a funeral wore sackcloth and ashes. In some Christian Churches today, the foreheads of worshipers are marked with ash on Ash Wednesday.

mentioned as the opponents of Jesus. What was meant was not, of course, the whole nation, but the leaders—Pharisees, Sadducees, priests, and so on.

The Gospels were written for Christians, who by that time included many Gentiles and who belonged to a new religion outside Judaism. Although the Gospel writers were Jews themselves (Luke may have been a Gentile), they tended to think of "the Jews" as the people who had opposed Jesus, as the Christian Church long continued to think.

Q What is the meaning of the name "Christ"?

A The name "Jesus" is a Greek version of the Hebrew name "Joshua," which means "God Saves." "Christ" is a Greek translation of the Hebrew word "Messiah," the exact meaning of which is "the anointed one." It came to stand for the expected Deliverer, or Savior, who was seen by many people at the time as a national hero like King David, a great king who would free the Jewish people from the disasters and ill fortune that had always afflicted them.

As far as we can tell from what the Bible says, Jesus became aware that he was the Messiah, or at least was someone like him, at the time he was baptized by John the Baptist. When, immediately after that, he went off into the wilderness where he was "tempted" (or tested) by the Devil, he was trying to understand exactly what his mission was.

Q What was the Transfiguration?
Matthew 17

A One evening, Jesus took Peter, James and John up into the mountains where they could be alone. Jesus began to pray, and while he prayed, he became transfigured, which means that his appearance changed. His clothes became a dazzling white; his face shone with a miraculous light. Two figures appeared and talked with him. They spoke of the fate that awaited Jesus in Jerusalem and of the way in which he would die.

Then a bright cloud appeared, covering the figures in a mist, and a voice was heard from the cloud: "This is my Beloved Son, whom I love. Listen to him." The three disciples covered their faces in fear, and did not move until Jesus came to them, touched them, and told them not to be afraid. The cloud had gone and the two figures had disappeared. When they left the mountain, Jesus told them not to tell anyone what they had seen.

Biblical scholars believe that the mountain on which this vision, called the Transfiguration, took place was Mount Hermon, near the town of Caesarea Philippi, a mountain high enough to have snow on the summit, on the present Lebanon/Syrian border.

Q Who spoke with Jesus during the Transfiguration?

A The two figures who appeared with Jesus in the vision of glory seen by Peter, James, and John were Moses and Elijah. These two great figures represented the Law (Moses) and the Prophets (Elijah), and their appearance with Jesus confirmed that he was in the line of the tradition of Judaism as it is described in the Old Testament.

Q What could be done with faith no bigger than a mustard seed?

A When Jesus and Peter, James and John came down from the mountain after the Transfiguration, they found the other disciples among a crowd trying to cure a boy who suffered with fits—probably epilepsy. They had been unable to cure him, or to "cast out the devil" in him, as people explained such troubles in those days.

The boy's father appealed to Jesus. Jesus said that everything is possible to someone who has faith. The man replied, in the words of the King James Bible, "Lord, I believe; help thou mine unbelief." (How many people since that time, troubled by religious doubts, have made the same prayer!)

When Jesus had cured the boy, his disciples asked him why they had not been able to do so. The answer Jesus gave them is rather different in Mark's and Matthew's Gospels. In Mark, Jesus tells them that more prayer is needed. But in Matthew's Gospel, he says that they must have more faith: "Even if you have faith no bigger than a mustard seed, you will still be able to move mountains."

Q What was the prayer that Jesus taught? Matthew 6, Luke 11

A The prayer which we know as the Lord's Prayer is the only one that Jesus himself taught. In those days, prayer was normally a public thing, and prayers were spoken out loud by a congregation—as the Lord's Prayer is today in Christian worship. That is why the prayer begins *Our* Father . . ."

The Lord's Prayer is a simple and beautiful

Mustard plants originated in the Middle East over 2,000 years ago. There were several varieties, including the black mustard and white mustard mainly used today.

prayer, but its precise meaning has been debated by theologians and Biblical scholars in many long and learned works. It appears in two different forms in the New Testament. The shorter version given in Luke's Gospel is thought to be the older. The extra piece at the end, "For thine is the kingdom, and the power, and the glory, for ever," which is in Matthew's version, may have been added later.

 Why did Jesus tell his disciples they must be like children? Mark 9

A On the way to Capernaum one day, the disciples were discussing among themselves who would be the greatest in the Kingdom of Heaven. They were still thinking of a political kingdom, and had not yet understood that Jesus would not be a king who rules, but one who serves his people. When they arrived at the house where they would be staying, Jesus asked them what they had been talking about. They were a little ashamed to admit it, but at last they asked him who would be the greatest among them in the Kingdom of Heaven.

There was a child playing nearby. Jesus called the child, put his arm around him, and said, "He who wants to be the greatest must make himself the least. Whoever does not accept the Kingdom of God like a child will never enter it." Once again, he was saying that the citizens of the kingdom of Heaven would be humble and child-like (but not childish!).

Jesus always showed his love of children: and he was practical too. When he brought Jairus' daughter back to life, he reminded her family that she first needed food (see page 145).

153

Q What is a millstone?

A Grain was ground into flour between two very large and heavy stones. The upper stone was turned with the aid of a handle, grinding the grain against the lower stone.

A millstone was therefore a very heavy object. Jesus said that, if any person destroyed the trust and humility of a child, it would be better for him if a millstone were hung around his neck and he were thrown into the sea to drown.

Q Why was Martha annoyed with her sister? Luke 10

A Mary, her sister Martha and their brother Lazarus were close friends of Jesus, and they lived in Bethany, a village near Jerusalem. Once, when Jesus was staying there, Martha—a good homemaker—was very busy cooking and cleaning, while her sister sat next to Jesus, doing nothing but listening to every word he said.

Understandably, Martha was annoyed with her sister for doing nothing while she was worked off her feet looking after Jesus and his disciples. At last she complained to Jesus himself, and asked him to tell Mary to give her some help.

Jesus smiled and shook his head. There was no need for her to work so hard, he said. The simplest meal would have been enough for him. Mary had chosen the most nourishing "food" by listening to his words. That should not be taken away from her.

Q What was the Sanhedrin?

A The Sanhedrin was the supreme court or council of the Jews, which met in a grand building near the Temple. Although it was mainly concerned with the Law, the Law could not be separated from non-religious matters such as politics. The Sanhedrin could punish people, and even have them executed, but to do that, it had to have the agreement of the Roman governor.

The Sanhedrin had about 70 members—mainly priests, Levites and the heads of the leading families (mostly Sadducees). In the time of Jesus, many of its members were Pharisees. However, it had authority only in Judea—not in Galilee. If he had wanted, Jesus could have avoided trouble with the Sandhedrin by staying away from Jerusalem.

Q Why did the Jewish leaders hate Jesus?

A Jesus was hated and feared by the Sanhedrin—the chief Jewish council—because in their eyes, he was a revolutionary. Of course, Jesus *was* a revolutionary of a kind—the greatest revolutionary in history—but his "revolution" was not the sort the Jewish leaders feared. The High Priest, Caiaphas, who was president of the Sanhedrin, put it something like this: "Here is this man—this Galilean—performing miracles and healing people all over the place. At this rate, the whole population will soon be treating him as the Messiah. What will happen then? The Romans will come and sweep away our temple and our nation. It is in our interest that this man dies, to save the whole nation from destruction."

Although Jesus had a few secret supporters even in the Sanhedrin (one of them was Joseph of Arimathea, who was to have the body of Jesus placed in his tomb after the Crucifixion), one fact which shows how much his influence was feared was the alliance between the Sadducees and the Pharisees. They were united in their hostility to Jesus, although they argued furiously about most other things.

Q What are phylacteries?

A Devout Jews wore little bags made of animal skin which contained passages from the Scriptures written on tiny pieces of parchment. One was worn on the head, and another on the left arm, so that, when the arm was folded, the bag was over the heart. These phylacteries were held on by leather bands. The band on the arm was wound around it seven times and then around the two middle fingers of the hand.

The phylacteries showed that the person wearing them devoted his head, hand and heart to God. They were not worn by women, nor

Phylacteries were one of the many ways in which strict Jews reminded themselves of their religious duties.

by boys under 13 years old. Some devout Orthodox Jews still wear them today.

In Jesus's day, they were normally worn only for morning prayers, but some people took to wearing them all day, or made the bands larger. This sort of behavior—"See how pious I am!"—used to annoy Jesus, and he had some sharp remarks to make about such people.

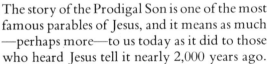

Who was the Prodigal Son? Luke 15

The story of the Prodigal Son is one of the most famous parables of Jesus, and it means as much —perhaps more—to us today as it did to those who heard Jesus tell it nearly 2,000 years ago.

"Prodigal" means wastefully extravagant, and the Prodigal Son was an example of a young man who could not wait to have a good time, who wanted to be rich right away. However, the point of the story is not so much the greedy and foolish behavior of the Prodigal Son, but the reception he got from his father when he returned, with no money and weak with hunger.

The story shows how God is overjoyed when a sinner repents. When the Pharisees used to criticize Jesus for mixing with poor sinners instead of respectable people like themselves, he used to say that it is the sick who need a doctor, not the healthy. And yet, of course, the

Pharisees themselves were "sick"—they were sick with the deadly sin of pride. They, too, needed to repent, and it was harder for them than for poor, humble folk.

What work did the Prodigal Son do when his money ran out?

The young man in the parable went off to a foreign country to have a good time, wasted all the money his father had given him, and then found himself in the middle of a famine. He managed to survive by taking a job as a pig-keeper, though he was so hungry that he was ready to share the pigs' food.

The job that the young man was forced to take would have seemed especially unpleasant to those who heard the story because pigs were "unclean" animals.

Pods of the carob tree, which the Prodigal Son fed to swine. The plant grows in very dry soil, and the pods, green at first, turn brown when they are ripe. Because they contain a rich, sweet, syrup, people eat them too.

Q What is the message of the lost sheep? Luke 15

A This is one of the parables Jesus told in answer to the scribes and Pharisees who criticized him for keeping company with poor folk and sinners. If a man has 100 sheep and one is lost, does he not go, Jesus asks, to look for it? And when he finds it, he is much more pleased about finding that one lost sheep than he is about the other 99 which never strayed. In the same way, God is happier over one sinner who repents than over 99 people who are not sinners, and do not need to repent.

The parable of the lost sheep was one of the ways in which Jesus tried to show the Pharisees and other self righteous people why it was natural for him to spend more time with "sinners."

Why did Zacchaeus climb a mulberry tree? Luke 18

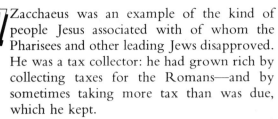

Zacchaeus was an example of the kind of people Jesus associated with of whom the Pharisees and other leading Jews disapproved. He was a tax collector: he had grown rich by collecting taxes for the Romans—and by sometimes taking more tax than was due, which he kept.

He lived in Jericho, and when Jesus visited that city, Zacchaeus wanted to see him very much. He had heard about Jesus, and what he had heard had moved him greatly. But many others also wanted to see Jesus, and Zacchaeus was a short man. He could not see over their heads, so he ran on ahead and climbed a mulberry tree from which he would be able to see Jesus. When Jesus passed, he stopped under the tree, looked up and said, "Zacchaeus! Come down, for today I am going to stay at your house."

What was the parable of the tax collector and the Pharisee? Luke 18

This parable was aimed, as Luke's Gospel tells us, at those who were confident that they were good people and therefore were entitled to look down on others.

Two men—a tax collector and a Pharisee—went to the Temple to pray. The Pharisee prayed: "I thank thee, God, that I am not greedy or dishonest, like other men—such as that tax collector there." The tax collector stood some way off and prayed: "God, have mercy on me, for I am a sinner."

It was the second man, said Jesus, who went home with his sins forgiven. But this teaching was something that the Pharisees, with one or two exceptions, could not accept.

Who was Tiberius Caesar?

The Emperor Tiberius (the title *Caesar* was adopted by all Roman emperors until Hadrian in the 2nd century AD), reigned from AD 14 to 37. He was therefore emperor during Jesus's mission and at the time of the Crucifixion—which he may never have heard about because,

to the Romans, Palestine was not a very important province.

His name is mentioned only once in the New Testament, when Luke's Gospel dates the beginning of the minstry of John the Baptist to the 15th year of Tiberius's reign. However, "Caesar," meaning "the Emperor," is mentioned many times.

Why did Jesus curse the fig tree? Mark 11

On his way from Bethany to Jerusalem, Jesus went up to a fig tree because he was hungry and hoped to find fruit on it. But it had no fruit, and he cursed it, saying, "May no one ever eat fruit from you again!"

This seems a rather strong reaction. Jesus certainly had a temper, but it usually only showed when there was something really worth being angry about. A wild fig tree could not be blamed for not having any fruit: sometimes such trees never bore fruit, and Mark says that it was not the right season anyway.

The story was probably told as a symbol of something else. The fig tree represented Israel, which had failed to produce fruit. The time had come for its destruction.

Why were the Jews "unfruitful"?

One theme of Jesus's teaching, which comes out most clearly in Matthew's Gospel, is that the Jewish people had failed to bring forth "fruit" (or a "crop"—the word is the same in Greek).

This goes back to the idea of the Covenant—the bargain between God and his Chosen People. God had kept his side of the bargain in giving them many blessings, but they had not lived up to their side. Therefore, Jesus says (Matthew, Chapter 21) that the Kingdom of God will be taken away from them and given to another people—in other words, the Gentiles.

In the other Gospels, Jesus seems to blame the Jewish leaders—the scribes, Pharisees and others—but in Matthew, it is a criticism of the whole people.

Q What is Palm Sunday?

A In Christian Churches, the last Sunday before Easter is known as Palm Sunday, in memory of the day when Jesus rode into Jerusalem at the beginning of the last week of his life. At that point, he was a very popular figure. His miracles, especially the recent raising of Lazarus, had made him famous, and he was greeted by a large crowd which strewed the ground in front of him with flowers and fronds from the palm trees.

Dried palm leaves commemorate the event today. In medieval England, when palms were not available, people used to make fronds from willows or other trees.

Q Why did Jesus ride into Jerusalem on a donkey?

A Outside Jerusalem, on the day that is remembered today as Palm Sunday, Jesus sent two of his disciples into the village of Beth-

Jesus enters Jerusalem on a donkey—an episode commemorated in the Christian Church on Palm Sunday.

phage, near Bethany. "You will find a donkey tethered there," he said. "Untie it and bring it to me. If anyone asks why you are taking it, say 'The Lord needs it,' and he will let it go."

As Matthew tells us, this was to fulfil a prophecy of the Prophet Zechariah: "See, your king is coming, mounted on a donkey." Matthew never missed making these connections with the Old Testament, in order to prove that Jesus was the Messiah. John also mentions Zechariah's prophecy, although Mark and Luke do not.

Q What kinds of shoes did people wear?

A Shoes or sandals were worn without socks or stockings. The usual sandals consisted of a sole of leather, fastened with leather bands which

went over the foot and around the ankle. Sometimes, sandals had hard soles with studs, for long journeys on rough ground. Others had soft soles of animal skin or even rushes or the bark from palm trees.

On entering a house, shoes were usually removed and the feet washed. People also often went barefoot, even outside. People in mourning always went barefoot.

Sandals were the normal footwear for everyone, from Roman governors to peasants, although most people often went barefoot.

Q **Whom did Jesus drive out of the Temple?**

A The Temple was the center of Jewish life, and it had also become a center for buying and selling, money-lending, trading and stealing. The Sadducees made a nice profit from the trade which they allowed to be carried on in and around the Temple. At festivals, the place was crowded with pilgrims, and there were plenty of opportunities for all kinds of cheating. The Temple tax had to be paid in Temple money, which meant that money changers were needed, and of course, they took every chance to cheat the simple pilgrims.

An old prophecy said that the Messiah would "clean" or purify the Temple, and this prophecy Jesus fulfilled with great ferocity, driving out the money changers and the traders with a homemade whip. "It is written in the Scriptures," he said, "that God's house shall be a house of prayer, but you have made it into a den of thieves!"

Q What did Jesus say about paying taxes? Matthew 22

A The Jewish authorities were eager to do away with Jesus, and that is why they asked him if it was right to pay taxes to the Roman Emperor. This tax was one that had to be paid by every citizen of Judea direct to the Emperor, and it had to be paid in Roman money.

It was extremely unpopular because it was a symbol of the Jews' submission to Rome. They always said that their loyalty was due, first and foremost, to God. The Jewish authorities were hoping to get Jesus into trouble with the Romans because they thought his answer would be "No." But if he said "Yes," he would have been in trouble with the Sanhedrin.

Jesus sent for a Roman coin and asked whose head appeared on it. "The Emperor's." "Give to Caesar what is due to Caesar and to God what is due to God," was Jesus's answer. They left him then, and went away.

Q Where did Peter find money for the Temple tax? Matthew 17

A The Temple tax was not very large, but many thought it should not be paid because there was nothing about it in the Law of Moses. When the tax collectors asked Peter if his master paid the tax, they were probably interested to know what Jesus, as a famous teacher, thought about this question.

Jesus and Peter were then on the way to Capernaum, and Jesus did not, at this point, want to cause trouble. So he told Peter to go and cast a line in the lake (the Sea of Galilee) and open the mouth of the first fish he caught. This Peter did, and inside he found, as Jesus had promised, a silver coin which was enough to pay the tax for both of them.

This sounds a little like a fairy story. It may have had more meaning for the early Christians, whom Matthew, the only Gospel writer to repeat this story, was addressing. Jewish converts to Christianity may have wondered whether they ought to go on paying the Jewish Temple tax. If this story about Jesus was their guide, the lesson was not to make a fuss about such a thing, but to pay up.

160

Q What was the Last Supper?

A The Last Supper was the Passover meal that Jesus ate with his disciples, the last meal before he was arrested (the arrangements for the meal were made in secret to prevent him being arrested earlier).

For Christians, this is one of the most important events in the life of Jesus, for it was then that he established the future form of Christian worship. It was then, too, that Jesus delivered his last message to his disciples, which is told in John's Gospel (Chapters 13–16).

The first Eucharist, or Mass. It was the custom for families and other groups to share a weekly meal at which the senior man would take bread and give thanks to God, and later do the same with a cup of wine.

Q What is the Eucharist?

A "Eucharist" means "thanksgiving" and it is one of the names given to the Christian ceremony first celebrated by Jesus at the Last Supper.

According to Luke's version, Jesus took a cup of wine and, after giving thanks, said, "Take this and share it among yourselves. For I shall not drink wine again until the Kingdom of God comes." Then he took some bread, gave thanks and broke it into pieces. He passed these among his disciples with the words, "This is my body."

In Mark's Gospel, Jesus broke the bread first and passed it to his disciples saying, "This is my body." Then he took the wine and all the disciples drank from the cup as Jesus said, "This is my blood, the blood of the covenant, which is shed for many." Matthew gives almost exactly the same account.

Q Why did Jesus wash the feet of his disciples? John 13

A During the Last Supper, the disciples, who still did not understand what Jesus meant by the Kingdom of Heaven, began to argue, as they had done before, over who would be the greatest in the new kingdom. Jesus told them how, in the Kingdom of Heaven, the greatest would be the least, and the ruler would be the servant. To demonstrate this, he took off his outer garment, tied a towel around his waist and, using a bowl of water, began to wash the feet of his disciples. This was a task that would normally have been done by the humblest member of the household.

When he came to Peter, the disciple objected. "Why should you wash my feet?" Peter asked. "I will not let you."

Jesus replied, "You do not understand yet, but later you will, for if you do not let me wash your feet, you are not in true fellowship with me." He was trying to explain that if he, their Lord, humbled himself in this way, they should surely be humble, too.

When he had finished, Jesus told them sorrowfully that one of them was going to betray him.

Q What was the reward for betraying Jesus?

A Jesus had been careful to give the authorities no chance to arrest him before he was ready, but he knew that Judas Iscariot would betray him. He told his disciples that the man who would do this was the man to whom he would give a piece of bread which he had dipped in the dish of food. He gave the bread to Judas.

The other disciples do not seem to have understood what was going on, and it was only at this moment that the idea of betraying Jesus came to Judas. John's Gospel says that as soon as Judas had received the bread, "Satan entered into him."

Judas immediately went out into the night to tell the chief priests where to find Jesus. His reward for this was "30 pieces of silver," quite a large sum (enough to buy a slave), although it is unlikely that Judas turned traitor just for the money.

Q Why did Judas Iscariot betray Jesus?

A Judas was probably one of the disciples who argued about who would be the greatest in the Kingdom of Heaven. Judas was thinking of a political kingdom—some scholars believe he may have been a member of the group called the Zealots, extreme Jewish nationalists who hoped to overthrow Roman rule.

Judas had been in charge of the disciples' financial affairs, and had been rather good at it. He was probably looking forward to a kingdom in which Jesus would be king and he would be in charge of the treasury. But by this time, he saw his dream slipping away from him. It seemed that there would be no kingdom of this sort. Jesus knew that he would become a traitor, but the other disciples never guessed. When Jesus told them that one of them would betray him, they all asked anxiously, "Is it I?"

Judas may have been hoping that, by betraying Jesus to the chief priests, he would force him to act—to lead a revolution, perhaps. He may have believed that Jesus would save himself by a miracle.

Q Where was the Garden of Gethsemane?

A After the Last Supper, Jesus went with his disciples to pray in the Garden of Gethsemane, where he was arrested. The Garden (probably an orchard) was on the Mount of Olives, which is really a small range of hills to the east of Jerusalem, separated from the city by the Brook of Kidron (Cedron). Jesus quite often went to the Mount of Olives in the evening, when other people had gone home. To reach Bethany, where he was staying, it was necessary to cross the Mount of Olives.

The spot where the Garden of Gethsemane is believed to have been still has groves of olive trees, some of them very old. The ground is now owned by several different Christian churches.

Gethsemane was a public garden, on the site of an old olive grove, only about one quarter of a mile from the Temple.

Q How did Jesus prophesy Peter's disloyalty?

A When they were on their way to the Garden of Gethsemane, Jesus told his disciples that, before the night was over, they would all betray him. Peter denied this hotly. Others might be disloyal, he said, but he never would. Jesus turned to him sadly and said, "Before the cock crows twice [that is, before the dawn], you will deny that you know me three times." Peter, almost in tears, refused to believe such a thing.

Q How did Judas identify Jesus?

A While Jesus was still speaking to his disciples in the Garden of Gethsemane, a crowd of men appeared: chief priests and elders (members of the Sanhedrin) and Temple police, who were responsible for keeping order in the Temple area. They were led by Judas Iscariot, who had no doubt guessed where Jesus would be because, according to Luke's Gospel, it was a place he often went to in the evening.

According to Matthew and Mark, Judas greeted Jesus with a kiss, which was the sign he had arranged with the chief priests to identify Jesus. According to Luke, Jesus was outraged and said to Judas, as he drew away from the traitor, "Would you betray the Son of Man with a kiss?"

Q What did Peter do when Jesus was arrested?

A When Jesus's disciples saw the approaching crowd of chief priests and elders, backed up by the officers of the Temple police, they realized what was about to happen and asked Jesus if they should use their swords to defend him. But one of them—perhaps Peter, who was always impetuous—drew his sword and cut off the ear of a servant of the High Priest.

The disciples' weapons would have been Roman swords—short and double edged. It is a little surprising that the disciples carried them, but they *had* been expecting trouble since they arrived in Jerusalem. In addition, Jesus had once advised them to sell their clothes and buy swords instead.

Jesus rebuked Peter for his action and healed the man's ear, although this detail is mentioned only by Luke.

Q Who escaped by slipping out of his clothes? Mark 14

A Slightly different accounts are given in the Gospels of the arrest of Jesus. There must have been other followers of Jesus besides the Twelve (actually 11 at this point) Disciples who were present. Mark and Matthew both tell us that when Jesus was arrested, and made no resistance, all the others ran away. (Luke does not mention this, probably because he did not want to put the disciples in too bad a light.)

According to Mark, among the followers of Jesus was a young man wearing a garment made of linen—a sign that he was reasonably well off. He was seized, but he slipped out of the loose-fitting garment and got away.

This vivid detail is not repeated by any of the other Gospels, and some people think the young man may have been Mark himself. However, that is only a guess.

Q Where was Jesus tried?

A Jesus was first questioned by Annas, the father-in-law of the High Priest, and a former High Priest himself, and then by Caiaphas, the current High Priest, who presided over the Sanhedrin, the supreme Jewish court.

The trial, held in the house of the High Priest, was not the sort that we are used to today. The chief priests and elders shouted at Jesus, mocked him, and hit him. All the same, there was no real evidence against him.

But finally, Caiaphas asked him straight out if he was the Messiah, and when he replied that he was, the High Priest shrieked, "Blasphemy!" He tore his robe as a sign of his disgust at such a claim, and asked for a verdict. "Death!" they all shouted.

However much they might wish to put Jesus to death, the Sanhedrin had no right to do so. Only the Roman authorities could do that, and it was necessary to get permission from Pontius Pilate, the Roman governor who was responsible to the Emperor.

Why did the maid servant think Peter was a follower of Jesus?

 When Jesus was arrested and taken to the house of the High Priest, Peter and John followed at a safe distance. They managed to get into the courtyard of the house, which was naturally a large one because the High Priest was the leader of the community. Many people were gathered there around a fire.

One of the High Priest's female servants asked Peter if he were not a follower of Jesus, but Peter denied this. As Peter left, the cock crowed. Then yet another maid saw him, and asked the same question. Again, Peter denied that he followed Jesus. A little later, another servant said that surely he was one of the followers, for he spoke as they did—it was Peter's accent that made them suspect him. He spoke in the accent of Galilee, where Jesus and nearly all of his disciples came from, which was quite different from the accent of Jerusalem.

Then Peter heard the cock crow again, and he wept as he remembered that Jesus had told him that before the cock crowed twice, he would deny him three times.

 Who was Pontius Pilate?

 Pontius Pilate was the Roman prefect, or governor, of Judea, and was directly responsible to the Emperor in Rome for the government of the province. He held his post for over ten years, from AD 26 to 36, which means he must have been a capable governor, as the Emperor did not tolerate failures. He was of Italian birth, a Roman citizen of middle-to-aristocratic rank, and it is likely that he had a good deal of experience as a soldier. He seems to have spoken with Jesus without an interpreter—probably in Greek. Although we know of a few other events in Pontius Pilate's career as prefect of Judea, we know little else, and today he is, of course, remembered simply as the man who sentenced Jesus to death.

 What happened to Judas?

 Judas Iscariot is, naturally, a hateful figure in Christian writings. He was one of the chosen Twelve, yet he was responsible for bringing Jesus to the Crucifixion by an act of treachery. To this day, to call someone "a Judas" is a fierce insult. However, Judas may have been not so much evil as mistaken.

When he saw that Jesus had been condemned to death, and realized that no miracle was going to save him, Judas was overcome with remorse and went to the Temple to return his reward of 30 pieces of silver to the chief priests. "I have sinned," he told them. "I have brought an innocent man to death." But they only laughed at him: "What is that to us?" Judas threw the money on the floor and left them. Soon afterwards, he was found dead—he had hanged himself.

Pontius Pilate and the High Priest. Although Pilate represented the supreme power, his chief concern was to keep the peace—even at the cost of executing a man unjustly.

Q Why did Pilate wash his hands?

A Pontius Pilate, as prefect of Judea, had to give his permission for Jesus to be executed. The priests accused Jesus before Pilate—of plotting against Rome and refusing to pay taxes, and of claiming to be a king. Pilate considered that Jesus was innocent of any serious crime, and was therefore unwilling to have him put to death. He tried several ways of saving him, but the Jewish leaders would have none of them.

There were great crowds in Jerusalem at Passover time. A riot would have been a disaster—certainly a disaster for Pilate's career —and he was unwilling to provoke the blood-thirsty leaders of the Sanhedrin. Not long before, he had annoyed the Jewish Elders by putting up some ceremonial shields. They had complained to the Emperor, and the Emperor had ordered Pilate to take the shields down again. He was very anxious not to cause more trouble, and therefore he let Jesus die. But he had seen Jesus privately and remained convinced of his innocence.

His final act in the case was to take a bowl of water and wash his hands in full view of the people, as a sign that he was innocent of shedding Jesus's blood.

Q Who was Barabbas?

A Pontius Pilate tried several ways of releasing Jesus, whom he considered innocent. One was to have Jesus released from jail by popular acclaim—a custom at this time of year, according to the Gospel writers.

A man called Barabbas was also in jail; he was a rebel and had been charged with murder. Pilate offered the people the choice of either Jesus or Barabbas. He was well aware that Jesus was more popular with the ordinary people than he was with the chief priests, and Pilate expected them to ask for him.

But the chief priests had been at work among the crowd that morning, and when Pilate asked who should be released, to his surprise they all shouted, "Barabbas!"

The name "Barabbas" means "Son of a father" (which is not very helpful) but apart from this incident, we know nothing more about him.

Q What was crucifixion?

A Crucifixion was the most horrible form of execution in the Roman empire, but it was not uncommon. It was the usual punishment for those who committed violent crimes. The cross may have been in the form of a T, or it may have been the type of cross that is usually shown in pictures of the Crucifixion. There was a support for the body either under the feet or between the legs, and the victim's arms were fastened to the cross-piece with nails. The victim was often flogged first, as Jesus was. This weakened him, and may have been meant to make him die sooner. Victims were also offered drugged wine, which was supposed to lessen the pain somewhat, but Jesus refused this.

Q What was the Place of the Skull?

A Outside Jerusalem, there was a round hill shaped like a human skull. It was called Golgotha, which means the "place of the skull," and it was here that the Crucifixion took place. The upright posts of the three crosses on which Jesus and the two outlaws were crucified were probably permanent fixtures. Crucifixions always took place outside the walls of a town or city, but near enough so that people would be forced to see them. They were intended as a warning to others as well as punishment for the victim.

Q Who carried the Cross?

A As was the usual practice, Jesus was forced to carry the Cross, on which he was to be crucified, to Golgotha. In fact, he probably carried only the cross-piece, as the main upright was permanently in position. Even so, it was a tremendous weight, and in his weakened state, after the flogging and the placing of the crown of thorns on his head, Jesus was unable to carry it. The Roman soldiers guarding him therefore stopped a man they met on the way and forced him to carry the Cross.

This man's name was Simon of Cyrene, and we know nothing more about him. He was no doubt a Jew and came from Cyrene in North

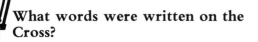

Africa. Mark mentions his sons, in a way which suggests that the readers of his Gospel would have known them. Possibly they—and their father—later became Christians.

Q | What words were written on the Cross?

A | When a man was crucified, there was often an inscription on the cross describing his crime, so that others would know why he had been

In his weakened state, Jesus was unable to carry the Cross, as those convicted were forced to do. Simon of Cyrene was probably picked by the guards because he was a well-built, strong-looking man.

condemned and would be warned against such a crime themselves. The inscription that Pilate had put on the Cross of Jesus was "This is Jesus the King of the Jews." The chief priests complained about this and said it should read, "This is Jesus who claimed to be the King of the Jews." But Pilate would not change it.

167

Q Who else was crucified with Jesus?

A Two criminals were crucified, one on either side of Jesus. One of them jeered bitterly at Jesus. "If you are the Messiah," he said, "why don't you come down off that Cross and save us as well?" But the other one stopped him. "We deserve our punishment," he said, "but this man has done nothing wrong." Then he asked Jesus to remember him when he came to reign as king. This shows that Jesus's message had reached many people, although the criminal was probably thinking of a great Jewish kingdom on earth rather than a heavenly kingdom of the spirit.

Jesus said to this man, "Today you shall be with me in Paradise," which was a greater favor than the man had asked.

Golgotha, or Calvary, the "Place of the Skull," was perhaps a burying ground for the poor, who had no one to give them proper burial. This would have made it convenient for the execution of criminals.

Q What did Jesus's words on the Cross mean?

A Before he died on the Cross, Jesus said several things, which the faithful watchers noted and remembered. When he was near death, he cried out, "My God, my God, why have you forsaken me?" Some people are troubled by what seems to have been Jesus's cry of despair. Had he lost faith in himself at the last moment? But this was not a cry of despair, it was a quotation from the Scriptures. The words come at the beginning of Psalm 22, which first deals with despair—and what could be seen as a prediction of Jesus's fate at the hands of humanity—and ends in praise and glory: "For kingly power belongs to the Lord, and he had dominion over all the nations." Jesus would have been thinking of that triumphant ending, not the despairing beginning.

Q | Who carried away the body of Jesus?

A | The bodies of those crucified had to be taken down before six in the evening, as that was the beginning of the Sabbath. The Roman guards hastened the deaths of the two thieves by breaking their legs. Because these could no longer support their bodies, they died of suffocation. Jesus was already dead, though a soldier drove a spear into his side to make sure.

Joseph of Arimathea went to Pilate and asked for Jesus's body. He was a member of the Sanhedrin, which shows that Jesus had followers even there. The Gospels make it appear that all the Jewish leaders were hostile to Jesus, but this was obviously not the case with Joseph —and there may have been other pious Jews

who shared his opinion. Together with another admirer of Jesus named Nicodemus, he took down the body from the Cross, washed and anointed it and wrapped it in a linen cloth. Then he placed it in a new tomb, perhaps one he had made in readiness for his own death.

Q What kind of graves were people buried in?

A In a hot climate, it was important to bury the dead quickly, usually within 24 hours of death. Coffins were not generally used in ancient Palestine; instead, bodies were placed in open graves and covered with stones. Wealthy people, like Joseph of Arimathea, had proper tombs made. The tomb Jesus was placed in was carved out of a rock in a cemetery.

Although we cannot now be certain, the tomb in which Jesus was placed is thought to have been located under what is now the Church of the Holy Sepulchre in Jerusalem, which was built by Helena, the mother of the Emperor Constantine, in the early 4th century.

Q Why were tombs sealed with a stone?

A Ordinary graves were covered with large stones, and a tomb carved out of the rock, such as that in which the body of Jesus was placed, had a large circular stone which was rolled in front of the entrance. The tomb in which Lazarus was buried was of the same type. The main purpose was to keep out wild animals, such as wolves, jackals, or dogs.

Accounts of the Resurrection given in the Gospels are rather confusing, so that it is not possible to follow the story exactly. However, all the Gospel writers agree in recording the vital fact that the tomb was discovered empty.

171

Why was the tomb guarded?

Although Jesus was buried secretly, several people found out where the tomb was, including the spies sent by members of the Sanhedrin. They were well aware that Jesus had promised to rise from the dead, and when they heard where his body lay, they went at once to Pilate and asked for a guard to be placed at the tomb —in case, they said, his disciples stole the body and then claimed that Jesus had risen.

The answer Pilate gave them was, "You have your guard." He may have meant that he would provide a guard of soldiers, as they requested, or simply that they had their own guards, such as the Temple police, and might use them. At any rate, a guard was placed at the tomb.

 What is the Resurrection?

"Resurrection" means "the return to life of the dead." Christians use the word for the return to life of Jesus after the Crucifixion. This is perhaps the most important single event in his life. It is possible to believe that the people whom Jesus is said to have raised from the dead were not, in fact, really dead—even Lazarus. Most Christian churches do not insist that their members believe in all the miracles related in the New Testament, but they must believe in the greatest miracle of all—the Resurrection of Jesus.

 What was the official explanation of the Resurrection?

Early on Sunday morning (the day after the Sabbath), the tomb in which Jesus had been placed was found to be empty. The four Gospels give slightly different versions of this, although the main events are the same.

The disciples of Jesus were slow to announce that Jesus had risen from the dead. Although he had promised that he would, the mere fact that the tomb was empty was not proof of the Resurrection, and their first reaction was not joy but consternation. Someone had taken the body away!

According to Matthew (other accounts are slightly different), Mary Magdalene and another woman came to the tomb about dawn, when there was a violent earthquake. An angel descended from Heaven and rolled away the stone which covered the entrance to the tomb. He sat down on the stone, his face as bright as lightning and his clothes white as snow. The guards shook with fear, then fell down as if they were dead.

Later, some of the guards returned to the city to tell the chief priests what had happened. A hurried meeting of the priests and Elders was called, and the guards were given a large bribe and told to say that the disciples of Jesus had come in the night, while they were asleep, and had stolen the body.

 Who first spoke to the risen Jesus?

When Mary Magdalene found the tomb empty, her first reaction was dismay. She ran to fetch Peter and John. According to Mark's Gospel, she was the first to see Jesus. While she was wondering what to do, he appeared nearby, although she did not recognize him at first. She thought he must be a gardener, and asked him if he knew where the body of Jesus had been taken. Then he spoke her name, and she knew who he was.

When the two disciples reached the tomb, John was the first to realize that Jesus had risen. He noticed that the cloth in which the body had been wrapped still lay on the shelf where the body had lain. If someone had taken the body away, they would not have removed the linen cloth and left it lying there.

 How did Thomas get his nickname?

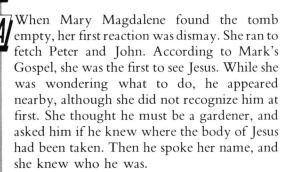We sometimes call a person a "Doubting Thomas," meaning he is one of those people who will not believe what they are told unless they have seen the evidence themselves.

In the evening of the day of the Resurrection, the disciples gathered together in secret— they were afraid of being arrested—to discuss the exciting news brought by Mary Magdalene. The doors were locked, yet suddenly Jesus was among them. "Peace to you all," he said, and sat down and ate with them to prove he was the real Jesus and not a ghost.

One of the disciples—Thomas—was away, and when the others told him what had happened, he would not believe it—"not until I can feel the marks of the nails in his hands and the wound in his side."

A few days later, Jesus appeared again among the disciples. He invited Thomas to feel the nail marks in his hands and the wound in his side. But Thomas was already on his knees, whispering, "My Lord and my God!"

 ## What is the Ascension? Acts 1

The Gospels come to an end with Jesus alive again among his disciples after the Resurrection. The story of the Ascension ("going up") is told in the first chapter of the Acts of the Apostles, a continuation of Luke's Gospel, in which the event is just mentioned.

Jesus still had much to teach his disciples, and they still had much to learn. They were still thinking of a splendid new kingdom here on earth, and believed that Jesus had only to show himself to the world, risen from the dead as he was, for that kingdom to come about. It was not until much later, when the Holy Spirit came upon them, that they really understood what the Kingdom of Heaven was.

Jesus tried to explain something of this to them on the last walk they took together, on the Mount of Olives. When he had finished speaking, a cloud came down and lifted him up to heaven. They stood staring up into the sky until an angel told them that Jesus had gone up to heaven, and would one day return in the same way.

Who is the Lamb of God?

According to John's Gospel, this was the name by which John the Baptist introduced Jesus after he had baptized him: "Behold the Lamb of God, who takes away the sin of the world!" In the Book of Revelation—the most difficult book to understand in the New Testament—the lamb is often a symbol for Jesus.

Lambs were the animals most often sacrificed, and Jesus himself was sacrificed—for the good of all human kind. At the Passover, a

The Lamb of God—the symbolic Jesus—in the stained glass of a church window

lamb was also the symbol of deliverance. Jesus also came to deliver human beings from evil.

In carvings and paintings made by the early Christians, the lamb was often used as a symbol, and in Christian Churches today, many prayers contain references to Jesus as the Lamb of God.

 ## Who was the 13th Apostle? Acts 1

Jesus had originally chosen Twelve Disciples. This was an important number, because of the 12 sons of Jacob who had founded the Twelve Tribes of Israel. After the death of the traitor, Judas Iscariot, there were, of course, only 11, and Peter thought they ought to choose another.

He should be someone who had been a follower of Jesus since the beginning of his mission, and their choice eventually lay between two men, Joseph, known as Justus, and Matthias.

The disciples prayed to God to guide their choice, which was made by casting lots—perhaps by writing the two men's names on pebbles, putting both into a bag, and taking out one without looking at the name.

Matthias was the chosen man. However, we know nothing about him except for this incident.

Who wrote the Acts of the Apostles?

The fifth book of the New Testament has a preface, or foreword, saying that it is a continuation of the Gospel of Luke. The preface is addressed to a man named Theophilus, as is Luke's Gospel, but even without this, scholars would have been able to tell that both Luke and Acts were written by the same man because of the style of the writing. Of Luke himself, we know almost nothing for certain. Tradition says that he was a Gentile, not a Jew, and that he was a physician, but there is no proof.

Luke did not give his second book a name, and it was not called the Acts of the Apostles until about 100 years later. While it does tell of the work of Peter and (especially) Paul, with whom Luke probably traveled, it does not say much about the other apostles. Its main subject is the beginning of the Christian Church.

What happened at Pentecost?

Pentecost was an old harvest festival, celebrated 50 days (which is what "Pentecost" means) after Passover. Although it was less important than Passover, many pilgrims came to Jerusalem to celebrate it.

After the Resurrection and before the Ascension, Jesus had told his disciples that in a short time they would be "baptized" by the Holy Spirit. This was the event that took place at Pentecost.

A large group of disciples and followers of Jesus were gathered in one room near the Temple. Suddenly there was a noise like a fierce wind, and a mass of fire, which separated into individual flames. A flame hovered over the head of each person there, and they were filled with an enormous sense of power and confidence. They also found they could speak foreign languages which they had never been taught.

The disciples ran out among the crowds and began praising God in the different languages that were spoken by the pilgrims. They were so full of enthusiasm that some people thought they were drunk. Finally, Peter made his great sermon, or address, in which he told the people to repent and be baptized in the name of Jesus. Some 3,000 people are said to have been converted. This marked the real beginning of the Christian Church.

When is Whitsun?

The Christian festival of Pentecost is often called Whitsun, which is short for "White Sunday." The name came about because of the white clothes that people wore to be baptized; this holiday was a favorite time for baptisms. (In the early Christian Church, only adults were baptized, not babies.) Whitsun is celebrated on the seventh Sunday after Easter, and the week following Whitsun is sometimes called Whitsuntide.

What is a tallith?

Every male Jew was supposed to wear the small tallith, which was a kind of loose undergarment worn next to the shirt. It had tassels and was usually blue. The large tallith was (and is) a kind of prayer shawl, worn at the synagogue. It was usually white, with black or

blue borders, and had a cord attached with eight threads and five knots to remind the wearer to obey the commandments of the Torah.

What did Gamaliel say in the Sanhedrin? Acts 5

 In the days after Pentecost, many were converted to Christianity by the preaching of the apostles. The Jewish authorities grew worried. They denied that Jesus had risen from the dead, as the apostles said, but they were unable to produce the body which would have proved it. Several times, the apostles were arrested, imprisoned, flogged, and then released. But the movement continued.

At least one member of the Sanhedrin argued against the persecution of the apostles. Religious movements like this come and go, he said. When their leaders die, the members are scattered and the movement dissolves of its own accord in a short time. That is what will happen with these people—unless their movement is inspired by God. And if it *is* inspired by God, it is better for us not to oppose it.

This man was a Pharisee named Gamaliel. Not all Pharisees were intolerant fanatics, as they sometimes seem to be in the New Testament. Gamaliel was a famous rabbi, who is also said to have been the teacher of Paul, although Paul, before he was converted, took a very different view of the Christian movement.

 What is a martyr?

The word "martyr" comes from a Greek word meaning "a witness." In the New Testament—which was, of course, written in Greek—the word was often used in this sense, meaning a witness to Jesus. The strongest form this witnessing could take was for a follower of Jesus to give up his or her life rather than give up his or her Christian faith. The word therefore came to mean one who sacrifices his life for his faith.

 Who was the first Christian martyr?

In the first little Christian community at Jerusalem which grew up after Pentecost, an argument broke out between Hebrew-speaking and Greek-speaking Christians. The Greeks said they were not being treated as equals, especially when the food was shared

out. The apostles appointed seven men to see that the food was distributed fairly, one of whom was Stephen. He was a powerful preacher, who had performed miracles, and could defeat the learned Jewish Elders in argument. He was brought before the Sanhedrin and charged with blasphemy. During his trial, he saw a vision and cried out, "I see the Son of Man sitting on God's right hand!"

This was more than the Sanhedrin could tolerate—Stephen had already accused them of murdering the Messiah. They dragged him out of the city—no executions could take place inside it—and stoned him to death. He was the first Christian saint to die for his beliefs.

 Who is a saint?

A saint is an especially holy person. In the Roman Catholic Church today, a saint can be created (perhaps centuries after his or her death) by an official process of the Church called *canonization*. However, in the Bible, the word "saint" is used differently.

In the Old Testament, a saint is any one of God's Chosen People. In the New Testament, a community of Christians might be called "saints." For example, Paul refers to the "poor saints at Jerusalem" in his Epistle to the Romans. More recently, some Christian groups, such as the Mormons, have called themselves a "community of saints." The idea of sainthood being something special began with the respect that was paid to martyrs in the early Christian Church.

It was not until about 500 years after the Christian Church began that "saint" became a special title of honor.

Q. Why were people killed by stoning?

A. Execution by stoning was a form of capital punishment which was approved by Jewish Law, especially for the crime of blasphemy. The Israelites did not like spilling blood, which they thought was a very special thing—the very soul, almost, of a man or animal. A man could be killed by stoning with no (or very little) blood being spilled.

Death by stoning had another advantage. It was not possible to say who had actually killed the victim, as all had taken part, and therefore no single person could be held responsible.

Q. Who was converted on the road to Damascus? Acts 9

A. One of the people present at the stoning of Stephen was a young Pharisee named Saul, who had been born in Tarsus (in what is now modern Turkey) and was a weaver by trade. He was also a Roman citizen, which gave him importance and some protection in his later missionary journeys.

Saul was one of the fiercest critics of the Christians, and after Stephen's death, the High Priest in Jerusalem sent him with orders to arrest Christians in Damascus (today the capital of Syria) and bring them as prisoners to Jerusalem. Since Pentecost, thousands had become Christians. When they fled from Jerusalem, however, they spread the good news about Jesus and the Resurrection.

On his way to Damascus, Saul was converted to Christianity by a vision. In it, the voice of God, coming from a blinding light, appointed him as his chief missionary to the Gentiles. Because of this special mission, he gave up his Hebrew name and took the Roman name Paul.

Paul is the most important person in the New Testament after Jesus himself. Some people have said that Paul was more important for Christianity than Jesus, though Paul himself would have called that blasphemous.

However, it was Paul, above all others, who transformed the small community of Palestinian Jews into a movement that spread into all parts of the ancient world and became the religion of all races.

N. Dear

The conversion of Paul on the road to Damascus was perhaps the most important event for the future of the Christian Church in the early days. Paul became the most powerful of the Apostles and he was mainly responsible for the spread of Christianity throughout the Roman Empire.

Q. How did Paul escape from Damascus? Acts 9

A. When Paul reached Damascus, instead of arresting the Christians there, he became one of them. He was soon appearing publicly in the synagogues, proclaiming Jesus—to the great astonishment of those who had heard of him only as a great persecutor of Christians.

He was a man of strong personality and also of great intelligence, and in his arguments with the Jews of Damascus, Luke says, he was easily

176

the victor. The leaders of the synagogues learned to hate and fear him. They plotted against his life, but Paul and the other Christians in Damascus learned of their scheme.

He had to get out of the city, but the authorities were keeping watch on all the city gates, so one night, Paul, hiding in a large basket, was quietly lowered down from the top of the wall in a quiet part of the city and so escaped.

Q Who are the Gentiles?

A Gentiles, which means simply "people" or "nations," was the name given by the ancient Hebrews to all non-Hebrew people. It is still used in that sense today, meaning "non-Jews."

The ancient Hebrews had kept their religion pure and had maintained their own identity (in spite of conquest, exile and other national disasters) by putting up a strong barrier against outsiders. A great deal of the Old Testament is about their success or failure in remaining "pure."

The attitude of Jesus was quite different. Galilee was, in any case, a region where many Gentiles lived, and Jesus never showed any prejudice against them, although he sometimes criticized them, and he did say that his mission was, first and foremost, to the people of Israel. He spent part of his time in Gentile regions, fulfilling the prophecy made by old Simeon in the Temple when Jesus was a baby, that he would "bring light to the Gentiles." This mission was taken up by Paul.

Q What was Peter's dream of unclean food? Acts 10

A Peter felt hungry and went up on the roof of a house to pray. There he had a vision in which a huge sheet descended filled with animals of all kinds, including reptiles, pigs, and other "unclean" animals. A voice said, "Get up, Peter. Kill and eat." Peter replied, "No, Lord. I have never eaten food that is unclean." God answered, "It is not for you to reject what God has offered."

Peter puzzled over the meaning of this. It was soon revealed when the messengers of Cornelius arrived at his house to say that their master wished to meet with Peter.

Cornelius was a Roman centurion, who was probably not a Roman citizen but was certainly a Gentile. He was sympathetic to the Jewish religion, and he too had received a vision in which he had been told to send for Peter. As a result, he became one of the first Gentiles to adopt Christianity. Peter, of course, recognized that his dream about unclean food had meant that, in spite of the Jewish restrictions against even talking to Gentiles, they were not to be rejected by those who followed Jesus.

Q How did Paul and Silas escape from prison? Acts 16

A On his second missionary journey, the Apostle Paul, accompanied by Silas, visited the Greek town of Philippi. They were followed everywhere by a slave girl who had the gift of prophecy. She would shout after them, "These men are the servants of God. They can tell you how to be saved." Paul grew tired of this and said, "Spirit, come out of that girl." She immediately lost the gift of prophecy, but this annoyed her owners, who had made a lot of money out of her prophetic sayings. As a consequence, Paul and Silas were dragged off to prison after being flogged at the order of the magistrates for disturbing the peace.

At midnight, the prison was shaken by an earthquake. The doors sprang open, and the chains on the prisoners fell off them. The guard, waking up, supposed the prisoners had fled, but Paul told him not to worry, they were still there. Meanwhile, the magistrates, having discovered that these powerful strangers were also Roman citizens, had become very nervous and, the next morning, ordered their release.

Q Why was a fish an early symbol of Christianity?

A In the early years of the Christian Church, especially in times when Christians were being persecuted, the picture of a fish was a secret sign of their faith. Its meaning was known only to Christians, who might draw a fish on the door of a house to tell other Christians that they would be safe there.

The letters which make up the Greek word for "fish" are also the first letters of the words "Jesus Christ, Son of God, Savior." However, we cannot be certain that this is the reason why the fish became a Christian symbol in the early days.

Q Where did Paul's travels take him?

A The missionary journeys of Paul take up a large part of the Acts of the Apostles, and we know almost exactly where he went. The map shows the outline of his missionary work in Asia Minor (roughly the same as modern Turkey) and the eastern Mediterranean, ending in Rome where he disappeared from history.

On his main journeys, Paul set out from Antioch, capital of the Roman province of Cilicia and Syria. The countries he visited were mainly inhabited by Gentiles, but there were often Jewish communities and synagogues in the cities. Paul usually had one or more companions on his journeys—Barnabas (on his first journey), Silas, Timothy, Titus, probably Luke, who recorded his work, and several others whose names are mentioned by Luke.

Q What is the meaning of the word "church"?

A The meaning of the Greek word which we translate as "church" is "a meeting of citizens." This is what the first churches were. Early Christians often had to meet in secret, usually

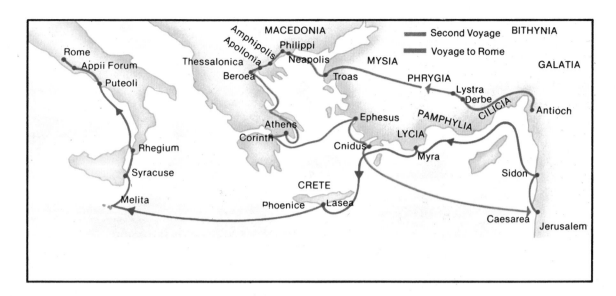

The map shows Paul's second journey and the route by which he eventually reached Rome. The probable reason why Paul's travels are so well recorded in Acts is that Luke was one of his traveling companions.

in the home of one of them. There was no special building, and the word "church" is not used to describe a building anywhere in the New Testament.

The word is used in two ways in the New Testament: either to describe a Christian group in one particular place, such as Corinth or Ephesus; or to describe all Christians who, although not yet united in a single organization, were seen by St Paul as one body.

What are the Epistles?

An epistle is simply a grand name for a letter. Out of the 27 books in the New Testament, 21 are epistles—letters written by apostles in the early years of the Church. A large number of them are said to have been written by Paul, and we can be fairly certain that many of these were. However, a few were not, just as the Second Epistle of Peter was not written until some years after the death of the Apostle Peter. The writer simply took Peter's name as a sign of respect for him.

Paul's epistles were not written with the idea of being published. They were greetings to churches he had founded, and they usually discussed some subject which was of special interest to that particular church. However, they have a universal value, too—in some cases, such as the Epistle to the Romans, a very great one.

Epistles are letters which, although they may be addressed to one person, are mainly about public affairs. In fact Paul often included personal messages in his epistles.

179

Where was Paul shipwrecked?

Paul's last journey was to Rome, as a prisoner. However, despite this, he was in very good spirits because it looked as though God's promise that he would preach the gospel in Rome itself was about to be fulfilled. His guard was a centurion named Julius, who respected him and treated him very well. Paul was able to visit many old friends on the journey.

After some days of difficult sailing, they reached Crete. It was late in the season, the stormy season was about to begin, and Paul advised Julius to wait in Crete. But the ship's master was not worried, so they put to sea against Paul's advice.

They were caught in a bad storm, which went on for days. The crew were very frightened, but Paul comforted them by saying that he had had a vision in which they all survived but the ship was lost. On the 14th night of the storm (this must be an exaggeration!), the ship was driven aground on the island of Malta, and broke up.

Paul's ship driven aground on the island of Malta. There were 276 people on board but, as Paul had promised, not one life was lost.

Who was Timothy?

We know that Timothy must have played a big part in helping Paul in his missionary work because he is mentioned as being with the Apostle in many of Paul's epistles. But we are not told much about him. He was the son of a Jewish mother and a Gentile father, and he sometimes acted as Paul's agent. A few remarks in Paul's epistles suggest that, at times, this may not have been an easy job.

There are also two epistles addressed to Timothy himself, but Bible scholars believe that these were written at a later time, long after the deaths of both Paul and Timothy.

Who thought Paul was a god? Acts 28

When Paul and his companions were shipwrecked on the island of Malta, the people there were kind to them and built a bonfire to keep them warm and dry their clothes. A viper, driven out by the heat, seized on Paul's hand. The islanders, knowing that Paul was a prisoner, said, "This must be a murderer whom the gods will not allow to live, even though he has escaped drowning." But Paul did not fall down dead, as they expected. Nothing happened to him at all, and the simple people then said to themselves, "He must be a god."

The viper was probably the snake known as an asp, which was quite common around the Mediterranean. Possibly it never actually bit Paul, but its bite could certainly be deadly.

What happened to Peter and Paul?

Paul eventually reached Rome safely. He lived there for about two years waiting for his appeal to be heard by the Emperor. Although still a prisoner, he was able to preach the gospel and to write several of his epistles. But what eventually happened to him, we do not know.

The book of the Acts of the Apostles also fails to tell us about the death of its other chief character, the Apostle Peter, but we do know that he, too, reached Rome, and it is likely that both men died when the Emperor Nero began to persecute Christians, about AD 64. Tradition says that Peter was crucified. The same is also said to have been Paul's fate, but as a Roman citizen, he was entitled to be executed by the sword.

Paul wrote to Timothy: "I have fought the good fight, I have finished my course, I have kept the faith."

The court of Nero. Roman emperors lived in the lap of luxury, which had a bad effect on an unstable character such as Nero.

Q Who was Nero?

A Nero became Roman emperor in AD 54. He was an example of the worst kind of emperor —so evil that he seems to have been insane. He was not especially hostile to the Christians— there were several among his own servants— but persecuted them when he felt like it. He tried to put the blame on them for the great fire which burned much of Rome in AD 64, and many Christians were then tortured to death. The Apostles Peter and Paul are believed to have died at this time.

The Senate, the body representing the most powerful Romans, finally lost patience with Nero and sentenced him to death, after choosing another emperor. Nero committed suicide in AD 68.

Q What happened to Jerusalem?

A Jesus lived in revolutionary times. Many people expected him to lead a rebellion against Rome, and after his death and Resurrection, rebellious feelings among the Jews did not cease. Finally, in the reign of the Emperor Nero, they had had enough. They threw out the Romans from Jerusalem and defeated a Roman force sent from Syria to crush them. They set up a revolutionary government which, for a short time, controlled most of the country.

Early in the next year, a much larger Roman army, commanded by two future emperors, entered Palestine. They soon regained control of the country and laid siege to Jerusalem. In the year AD 70, Jerusalem fell, and terrible cruelty and destruction took place. The Temple was destroyed, never to be rebuilt, and the Jewish state ceased to exist.

Q What is the Wailing Wall?

A There is in Jerusalem today a high stone wall, made out of huge blocks, which is said to be all that remains of the Temple which was burned in AD 70. It became a tradition for Jews to gather there on the eve of the Sabbath to pray. Pious Jews still pray there.

Q What is the Revelation of St John the Divine?

A The Book of Revelation is the last book of the New Testament. It is hard to understand, as it is not a story or teaching but the vision of a poet. It is sometimes also called the Apocalypse, a form of writing which is not found very much in other parts of the New Testament but is more common in the Old Testament (for instance, in the Book of Daniel).

Revelation is full of symbols—seven-headed dragons and so on—but its subject is simple enough. It is about the struggle between good and evil, and the coming of Christ and his kingdom, which the author believed would happen soon.

Q Who was St John the Divine?

A This is the name of the author of the Book of Revelation, the last book of the New Testament. "The Divine" means only "the theologian," and we do not know who this "John the theologian" was. It is agreed by Bible scholars that he was not the same man as the author of John's Gospel, although both books were written about the same time. Nor is it likely that he was the Apostle John.

The author was a prisoner on Patmos, an island about 50 km (30 miles) off the coast of what is now Turkey, when he had the visions which his book describes. He wrote them down to encourage his fellow-Christians at a time of danger and persecution.

The risen Christ—symbol of hope for the thousands of poor people who became Christians in the 1st century AD.

Q When was the Bible translated into English?

A The Bible has been translated into more than 1,000 languages. Most of this has happened in the last 200 years. The need of Christian missionaries to teach the Scriptures was often the reason for making a written version of languages which existed only in spoken form, especially in Africa.

Many translations of the Bible into English were made in the Middle Ages, though most of them only covered part of the Bible. It was not until the 16th century that a true English Bible was produced. That was the translation of William Tyndale, who published his version of the New Testament in 1525–6. He later translated part, but not all, of the Old Testament.

A number of other translations were made soon afterward, but they were not very good ones. Either they were incomplete, or they relied on other translations, not on the oldest Greek or Hebrew texts which were available. A new English Bible was needed, and it was produced in 1611 in the Authorized Version, which is also called the King James Bible. It was dedicated to King James I of England, who had commissioned it. Written in the language of Shakespeare—he was writing his finest plays about the same time—this has been the most widely used Bible in English. It is still read—and used in churches—today, although there are many more modern translations that are often more accurate, although they are perhaps less inspiring.

 What is the New Jerusalem?
Revelation 21

The vision of the New Jerusalem

 In a dream, the author of the Book of Revelation saw the Holy City, the new Jerusalem, coming down out of heaven—a city which needed no sun or moon for it was lit by the glory of God. The gates of the city were always open because nothing evil could ever enter it.

This is the heavenly Jerusalem—there was no longer an earthly Jerusalem because the Romans had destroyed it. It is a vision of eternal peace, a return to the Garden of Eden,

where humanity was perfect. It is, in a way, the dream of everyone.

This vision, related by an old man nearly 2,000 years ago, has tremendous power. This is partly because the writer was inspired by his belief in the victory of Jesus over the evils of the world. He believed that the heavenly kingdom was coming soon—very soon. But it has not come yet.

186

Index